Managing Rural Development
Ideas and Experience from East Africa

Managing Rural Development

Ideas and Experience from East Africa

by

Robert Chambers

The Scandinavian Institute of African Studies
Uppsala 1974

© 1974 Robert Chambers and Nordiska afrikainstitutet
ISBN 91-7106-075-8
Printed in Sweden by
Bohusläningens AB, Uddevalla 1974
ALLF

Contents

Preface and acknowledgements

This book has been written for those concerned with the policies, practice and study of rural development in the third world. It is addressed to political leaders, planners, civil servants, government field staff, the staff of institutions which train for the public service, aid agency and technical assistance personnel, and teachers and students of disciplines concerned with rural development.

The persistent disappointments in the planning and implementation of rural development programmes and projects are notorious. So too are the difficulties in shifting a larger and fairer share of resources to the rural sector. There has also been a widespread tendency for policies, whatever their original intentions, to be bent and altered in implementation so that they disproportionately benefit those who are already better off. The main thrust of this book is that to correct these imbalances and to improve performance a key but neglected means is presented by management procedures.

The ideas and experience are drawn mainly from Eastern Africa, including Kenya, Uganda, Tanzania, Zambia and Botswana. Much of the experience is derived from the Kenya Government's Special Rural Development Programme. So that the lessons can be used elsewhere, an attempt is made to extract some general principles and precepts. Recent experience in India and Sri Lanka encourages me to believe that they may be very widely applicable. I hope, therefore, that they will come to be of use to those working in rural development not only in Eastern Africa but also elsewhere wherever rural development is a priority.

Most of the approaches and methods which are described and discussed could be used to serve different policies to benefit different groups of people in different ways. In that sense they might be considered value-neutral. But I have gone beyond this and have sometimes indicated what I think *ought* to be done. I hope it will be clear to the reader when I am doing this. Social scientists often cloak their value judgements with words like "functional", "appropriate", "beneficial", "positive", "constructive" and "supportive" and their opposites. I have sometimes used "good" and "bad". I hope the reader will not be put off by this. For I do not think that the values which underlie the judgements and preferences expressed are very unusual. They include the belief that it is good to remove avoidable privation and suffering, to widen the choices and experiences which are open to people, and to improve the quality of life. In the context of rural development these apply particularly strongly to those who are worse off.

To speed up the achievement of these values I believe that there is a case for diverting resources and ingenuity to improving the management of government organizations in rural areas. But whether the potential of this approach can be realized depends critically upon a powerful and consistent supporting political will. By showing just a little of what might be done, I should like to hope that this book will influence what it is decided to try to do. I should like to believe that it will make it easier, even if only in a small way, to shift resources to the rural sector and to get through to more of those rural people who are worse off, helping them to help themselves. Perhaps these hopes are fond delusions. If they are, the work may still have been justified if it at least provides some leads and points of departure for others who then, as I hope, will supersede it with better informed, more perceptive and above all more usable work.

There is no pretence here to finished or final answers. Some stages of experiment, comparison and analysis are reported on. Some of the experiences—with the programming and implementation management system described in Chapter 2, and with the field staff management system described in Chapter 3—have not been easy to write up. This has been for two reasons: first, as one of the two main designers of these systems (the other being Deryke Belshaw) I know I am liable to bias; second, at the latest stage described, both systems were still evolving, with their futures uncertain. These might have been reasons for waiting and for encouraging someone else to evaluate them and write them up later. But I thought it might help others to know without such delay something of the winding path we followed, the mistakes we made, and the conclusions we were driven to. They may then be able to follow quicker and more direct paths. Later perhaps someone else will see what happens to these systems—whether they quietly wither away, are formally abandoned, stagger on as mechanistic rituals, or are usefully developed and replicated—and describe the lessons to be learnt.

The systems reported in this book and the ways of thinking that

8

underlie them owe a great deal to Deryke Belshaw. I am very deeply indebted to him for our collaboration during the period when we were both associated with the Institute for Development Studies at the University of Nairobi. In particular, it was he who explored and sharpened the systems thinking approach and pushed it into a number of fields which are not described here. He was responsible for the identification of the six clusters of procedures. Parts of Chapters 1 and 2 draw on material from papers of which we were co-authors and which are referred to in the text. He had a major part in devising, developing and introducing the PIM and field staff management systems reported in Chapters 2 and 3 respectively. It was also he who thought of and convened the rural research and development committees described in Chapter 5 and who did most of the work on evaluation procedures. In the event, with our largely unsynchronised movements in different continents, it has proved more practicable for us to present our interpretations separately. I have therefore written this book and accept responsibility for the views expressed in it. The joint nature of the research is, however, recognized in the use of the first person plural in the text. It remains a pleasure as well as a duty to acknowledge my considerable intellectual and practical debt to him.

The SRDP experience and the development of management procedures within the SRDP were only possible through the goodwill, tolerance, enthusiasm and imagination of many people, both Kenya Government officials and colleagues in the University of Nairobi. The greatest debt is to James Leach for his outstanding service to Kenya in pioneering the SRDP in the face of many difficulties, for his consistent support for the development of management procedures, and for his practical and constructive criticisms and suggestions. The PIM system was developed with his help, and with that of many others including Eric Crawford, John Gerhart and W. P. M. Saisi. The first four Area Coordinators—J. K. Okidi, J. A. Omungo, W. P. M. Saisi, and B. G. K. Wanjala—accepted the system, put it into practice, modified it and made it work. The many others who contributed included Provincial Planning Officers and David Brokensha, J. Caudle, H. H. A. Chabala, J. Tait Davis, J. Mugo Gachuhi, D. H. Kiiru, David K. Leonard, Peter Moock, S. W. Mukuna, James Mwaniki, John Nellis, Henry Ogola, W. Ouma Oyugi, Peter Wass and Carl Widstrand. The agricultural field staff management systems could not have been developed without the full collaboration of the Embu District Agricultural staff. Thanks are particularly due to John Magajo, the Assistant Agricultural Officer in charge of Mbere Division, for his hard work and patience, and to the staff under him for persevering through the experimental stages. Useful refinements were added by Chris Trapman. The community development system was identified with the help of Esther Keli. Many people took part in the exploration of area plan formulation procedures and Nilam Bedi and Jess Hungate contributed directly to a draft planning manual, the main part of which was the work of Deryke Belshaw. I should also like to express my gratitude to those in Botswana, Tanzania and Zambia who made my visits there so enjoyable and useful, to Carl Widstrand and the Scandinavian Institute of African Studies for hospitality and the organization of the seminar on the management of rural development held in Uppsala in April 1973, and to the participants in that seminar for the opportunity to try out some of the arguments presented in this book and to benefit from their ideas and criticisms.

All of these people, and many others not mentioned, played their part in generating and giving form to the ideas and experience presented and discussed in this book.

The Rockefeller Foundation funded the post I held at the Institute for Development Studies when some of the fieldwork was done and the Overseas Development Administration of the British Government through the Institute of Development Studies at the University of Sussex provided me with a six months' grant at short notice to enable me to travel, finish off the field work, and write up. During that period the Director of the East African Staff College, Ron Roper, generously gave me a place to work in a congenial atmosphere.

An early draft benefited from comments by Deryke Belshaw on the first four chapters and the first part of Chapter 5, by David K. Leonard on Chapter 3, and by W. Ouma Oyugi on Chapter 4. The resulting revision was fair typed at extraordinary speed through the good offices of Barry Peters at the Institute of Development Studies at the University of Sussex where it became a Discussion Paper. Substantial revision of that draft was made following reflection and in the light of valuable comments by James Leach, John Nellis, and Carl Widstrand on the whole manuscript. While I was writing my wife Jennifer bore with me beyond the limits of a reasonable interpretation of the marriage vows and later helped to correct my English. To all these people I am grateful for their help and for their perceptive and painstaking criticism. For the errors of judgement, fact and style which remain I am of course solely responsible.

Robert Chambers

I. Points of Departure and Directions

Dr. Kenneth Kaunda, President of the Republic of Zambia, introducing the Second National Development Plan 1972—1976:

"For us, developing the rural areas is a matter of life and death, though we do not underestimate the problems involved . . .
. . . We must first of all succeed in developing the rural areas, no matter what our performance is in other sectors."

(Republic of Zambia, 1971: (iii) and (iv))

Sir Seretse Khama, President of the Republic of Botswana, introducing the National Development Plan 1970—75:

"The greatest challenge ahead of us is undoubtedly that of rural development. The transformation of rural communities everywhere presents an intractable problem . . . Yet if the majority of Batswana are to benefit from the dramatic increase in the pace of development which has taken place since Independence, this problem must be solved."

(Republic of Botswana, 1970)

Mwalimu Julius K. Nyerere, President of the United Republic of Tanzania, introducing the Tanzania Second Five-Year Plan, 1969—74:

"This decision to give top priority to rural development does not only affect what is done in the rural areas; it also has implications for every other aspect of the Development Plan."

(United Republic of Tanzania, 1969: (xvii))

Republic of Kenya, Development Plan 1970—74:

"The key strategy of this Plan is to direct an increasing share of the total resources available to the nation towards the rural areas."

(Republic of Kenya, 1969:4)

1. The priority of rural development

The arguments for giving priority to rural development in the countries of Eastern Africa, as in most of the less developed world, are powerful and widely accepted.

First, and most obviously, the majority, and usually the overwhelming majority, of the people live and find their livelihoods in the rural areas. In Eastern Africa the proportion of the population described as rural varies, with according to official statistics 97 per cent in Burundi (1970), 95 per cent in Tanzania (1967), 95 per cent in Uganda (1969), 90 per cent in Kenya (1969) and 70 per cent in Zambia (1971). In all these countries, even Zambia with its atypically high level of urbanization, the absolute numbers of people living in the rural areas are expected to go on increasing for many years.

Second, the drift to the towns is a matter of concern. The high costs of urban housing and services, the health hazards of shanty towns, the security and political aspects of a large body of urban unemployed, and sometimes the adverse economic effects of rural depopulation —these are all reasons put forward for wishing to restrain urban growth; and one way of achieving this is seen to be the promotion of additional income and employment opportunities in rural areas.

Third, it is in the rural areas that most of the poorer and most disadvantaged people are to be found. Equity has been a recurrent theme in the speeches of some African leaders, most notably Nyerere, Kaunda, and Seretse Khama, and it is in line with this concern that the report of the ILO Mission to Kenya in 1972 was entitled "Employment, Incomes and Equality" and included proposals for target minimum rural incomes (ILO 1972:316—318). Increasing attention has been directed to the very poor often malnourished people who live almost invisibly in pockets of poverty in the rural areas. They are precisely the people who are least in contact with the modern world, least influential politically, least likely to possess adequate land and capital for a decent life, least able to help themselves, and hardest for governments to help. In contrast, the urban poor and unemployed, by virtue of the very fact that they have usually migrated from rural areas, are often the more energetic and able-bodied members of the population, while it is often the widows, the deserted wives, the old, the feeble and the very young who remain behind. The quickening concern for the "poverty of the poorest 40 per cent of the citizenry", in Robert McNamara's phrase (1972:9), can be expected to continue to reinforce

12

the priority for rural development since it is in the rural areas that the great majority of these people live.

Fourth, there is a cluster of now orthodox economic arguments for giving priority to rural, and particularly agricultural, development. The strange errors of economists after the Second World War, with their belief in industrialization as the prime strategy for underdeveloped countries, have passed into history. The importance of self-sufficiency in food in order to save foreign exchange and to keep down urban wages; the need to develop cash crops in order to earn foreign exchange, particularly in those countries which lack minerals or oil for export; the existence of underexploited land and labour which can relatively easily be brought into production; the desirability of increasing rural purchasing power to provide markets for the new urban products—these are among the most persuasive economic reasons for the shift of priority towards agricultural development, reasons which seem unlikely to lose much of their force during the next decade and perhaps for much longer.

A government which accepts these arguments has many choices of strategies for improving rural life. It is all too easy to think almost exclusively in terms of action through government administration. Since the management of such action is the main focus of this study, it is salutary to make clear at the outset that there are many fiscal devices which can also be used and which often, but not always, are sparing in their demands on administration. Perhaps the easiest and most administration-sparing is devaluation, which raises the prices paid for export crops and hence may raise returns to the farmers who grow them (who tend, however, to be those who are already better off) and which simultaneously raises the price of imports including luxuries on which more prosperous urban dwellers rely more heavily. Indeed, one major motive for the East African devaluation of February 1973 was precisely the benefits which would accrue to the rural sector. Many other measures may also be administration-sparing to varying degrees, including subsidies for agricultural inputs, support prices for agricultural produce, tariff protection against cheap food imports, and tax incentives for rural investment, among others. Measures of these sorts deserve very serious consideration, some of them especially in those countries like Botswana and Zambia where a mining sector generates substantial government revenues which can be channelled into the rural areas. They initially tend to favour those rural people who are already better off; but they do at least increase rural incomes with the possibility of spread effects which may create additional rural employment and the further distribution of incomes in the rural sector.

A major, perhaps the major, means of government intervention to promote rural development and welfare is, however, through government administration—especially in fields such as education, health, communications, water supplies, co-operatives and marketing, credit, agricultural research and extension, family planning, nutrition, and various forms of production infrastructure. The record here is one of mixed successes and failures, with many frustrations and disappointments. In order to try to see a way forward to improvements, a first step is to review some of the main features of the experience which has already been gained.

2. Experience

In the countries of Eastern Africa there has been a wide variety of government initiatives and approaches in rural development. Any attempt to classify these quickly runs into difficulties, but can be made clearer by a definition of terms. For the purposes of this book the following conventions are followed:

sector and *sectoral* are used to refer to a focus of development activity for which there is typically a separate specialized government organization (such as agriculture, education, health, water supplies, roads);

project is used to refer to a set of organized development initiatives confined to or considered in relation to a low-level administrative or geographical area;

programme is used to refer to a set of development initiatives planned for, undertaken in or affecting several or many low-level administrative or geographical areas.

A programme may thus consist of a number of projects, and a project may be part of a programme. An isolated project may, however, exist without a programme.

Using these terms in these senses, most government rural development initiatives and approaches can conveniently be classified by territorial and organizational criteria into three groups: programmes and projects which are multi-sector and have bounded sites; sectoral programmes; and area management. A brief review of the nature and performance of these three groups will provide some necessary background for the arguments which underlie the themes of later chapters.

(i) Multi-sector bounded-site programmes and projects

Much attention has been attracted by programmes and projects which involve intervention in more than one sector and which are confined to particular sites. Of all rural development initiatives they have tended to be the most visible, the most visited, the most researched and the most written about. They include many settlement schemes, various projects of the World Bank, and the programme of *ujamaa vijijini* in Tanzania. (Plantations and state farms are not considered here since they are generally mono-sectoral, focussing on the agricultural sector). Typically a special organization is created and there is a clearly defined geographical and organizational entity at the local level. Typically, also, official objectives include both economic and welfare goals.

Until recently almost all of these programmes and projects have been created as a result of an administration-intensive approach initiated by government or by a donor agency. Examples are: in Tanzania the mechanized settlement scheme at Nachingwea (Lord 1963) which followed the Groundnut Scheme (Wood 1950) (which latter was, however, a state farm), and the post-Independence Pilot Village Settlements (Ellman 1967; Georgulas 1967; Landell-Mills 1966; Nellis 1967, 1972 c; Newiger 1968; Rweyemamu 1966; Thomas 1967); (for a fuller bibliography, see Chambers and Moris 1973: 517—8); in the Sudan, Gezira (Gaitskell 1959, Shaw 1967) and the Zande Scheme (Reining 1959, 1966); in Kenya the irrigation schemes of the National Irrigation Board including the Mwea Irrigation Scheme (Chambers 1969 a; Chambers and Moris 1973) and the Million-Acre Settlement Scheme (Chambers 1969 a for bibliography and Maina and MacArthur 1970, Mercer 1970); in Ethiopia, the Chilalo Agricultural Development Unit (CADU) (Nekby 1971); and in Uganda, the Nyakashaka settlement for school-leavers (Hutton 1970, 1973) and the Mubuku Irrigation Scheme (Gitelson 1971). Much attention has also been attracted by the bounded-site projects of the World Bank such as those at Lilongwe and Karonga in Malawi and in the Western State Lands of Botswana.

Organizationally these programmes and projects have almost without exception had three characteristics in common. First, management has been centralized and technocratic, and "success" has been sensitive to the managerial skill of men such as Gaitskell at Gezira, Carr at

Nyakashaka, and Giglioli at Mwea. Second, where "successful" the organization has been largely independent of local field administration and protected from outside interference either by high political priority or by isolation from political influences. Third, in their genesis to date there has been a strongly expatriate input in management and often in capital. These three characteristics have been related to the value and limitations of multi-sector bounded-site initiatives. On the positive side, some outstanding contributions have been made to rural development. The Gezira Scheme has provided a backbone for the economy of the Sudan but is an exception to most generalizations. Other projects have developed techniques which have then been replicated. For example, CADU in Ethiopia generated the minimum extension package programme which was then spread widely outside the original project area; Nyakashaka in Uganda developed an approach to school-leaver settlement which was subsequently repeated elsewhere; and Mwea in Kenya pioneered a technical and management system for paddy-growing which was then transferred to other irrigation projects. On the negative side administration-intensive site-bound projects have often failed. They are vulnerable to the calibre of management. The combinations of local political isolation, high-level political priority and expatriate management have contributed to their instability. Most seriously, the benefits which derive from them have been limited to the small populations immediately involved. Through special inputs these projects may be made to work; but the vast majority of the rural population of the country is usually unaffected in any positive way.

A contrast is provided by the programme of *ujamaa vijijini* in Tanzania (Nyerere 1968; Proctor, ed. 1971; Cliffe and Saul 1973; Temu 1973). With its intention of affecting many in the rural areas and its apparently administration-sparing self-help ideology, it differs in its rationale from earlier approaches. Management is decentralized and democratic; villages exploit their political priority as a means of securing government resources and services; and they are incontrovertibly Tanzanian in management and character. A further difference is the large numbers of people who are stated to be living in *ujamaa* villages, official statistics giving just over 2 million at 31 May 1973 out of a population of 13 million in Tanzania as a whole (Temu 1973:72). Some of these impressions are, however, probably deceptive. Some *ujamaa* villages, by attracting government services and capital, may well be or become as administration-intensive as some of their settlement scheme precursors. The observer may also be justified in treating the official statistics with as much scepticism as those registering achievement in any other dispersed programme which has high political priority and on the performance of which civil servants and local leaders believe they will be judged. It is too early definitively to evaluate the *ujamaa* programme though not too early to try to find out whether or to what extent it reaches and benefits the less well off people in rural areas. Even if it has substantial benefits in helping the disadvantaged, however, it still suffers from the basic disadvantage of most bounded-site programmes: that resources and services with high opportunity costs are liable to be concentrated on a small fraction of the population. This does not necessarily invalidate the approach. It does, however, suggest that it is no panacea and that other approaches are also needed and will continue to be needed to reach the great majority of a rural population.

(ii) Sectoral Programmes

In terms of their total actual and potential contribution to rural development and welfare, sectoral programmes are more important. They include all the programmes of specialized departments of government and parastatals which are not multi-sector bounded-site programmes or projects. Programmes for roads, rural water supplies, health facilities, agricultural extension, adult literacy, family planning, home economics and nutrition, forestry, education, and community development are examples. Typically, specialized trained staff who work within independent departments are responsible for these programmes. Typically, too, they are either national in their spread or they include a wide spread of areas. They also absorb a high proportion of the recurrent budgets of the countries of Eastern Africa.

Three criticisms commonly levelled at sectoral programmes deserve particular attention. The first is a failure to spend effectively the development funds voted for them. This was a serious problem in the first years of the First Tanzania Development Plan in the mid-1960's when "mistakes were made at the outset of the Plan in underestimating implementation bottlenecks" (United Republic of Tanzania 1969:16). This led to under-investment, although performance subsequently improved. A further example was the rural water development programme in Kenya which in 1969/70 was able to spend only somewhat less than half of the sum voted (Republic of Kenya 1971b:243). In such circumstances it is the executive capacity of departments rather

17

than official plan and budget allocations which determines the actual investments which take place. A second criticism, which we shall consider later (see pages 57 to 61), is that field staff, particularly those right at the bottom of the hierarchy, are idle, incompetent and ineffective. A third criticism is that sectoral programmes are often uncoordinated, resulting in duplication, gaps, poor timing of inputs which should be phased and complementary, and confusion for the people.

Nevertheless, the importance of sectoral programmes, co-ordinated or not, is easily underestimated because they so often continue quietly without a fanfare, without a geographical focus which attracts visitors, and without the attentions of research students. The management of central government field agencies has also assumed greater significance in Kenya, Tanzania and Zambia as local authorities have had their most important responsibilities (for primary education, roads and health in both Kenya and Tanzania) removed from them. The sums of money involved in sectoral programmes are very large and the field staff often very numerous. Management for the effective deployment of such large investments in rural areas can scarcely fail to deserve a very high national priority.

(iii) Area Management

The third category of rural development initiatives can be described as area management, defined as procedures which combine the staff of different departments in an administrative area in the common management of development work. Examples are development committees, block grants allocated to development committees, decentralization on the Tanzanian and Zambian models, and the formulation and implementation of plans for particular areas.

Again, experience has been mixed and often disappointing. In the 1960's Development Committees at Provincial or Regional and also District level were set up in Kenya, Uganda, Tanzania, Zambia, Malawi and Botswana. (For a fuller description and analysis see pp. 88—94.) They suffered variously from being huge political forums, with attendances in three figures; from long discussions of their members' complaints about housing and conditions of service; from uncertainty about their functions; and from lack of authority and lack of control of resources. At their worst they either failed to meet, or if they did meet, wasted time. But on the positive side, when they were reasonably small in membership and when their advice and opinions were taken into account, they were sometimes lively, active and responsible bodies. When they were given block votes to allocate the results were patchy: committees were made active by having resources to dispose of, but sometimes there was substantial corruption. In Tanzania the Regional Development Fund, as the block vote was called, was overtaken in 1972 by a radical decentralization in which many staff were posted from Dar es Salaam to the regions, budgetary authority was substantially devolved to the regions within limits set by central ministries, and Regional Development Directors and District Development Directors were appointed as managers of the technical staff in their areas. In early 1973 Zambia was beginning to implement a somewhat similar decentralisation which had earlier been agreed in principle. The Tanzanian decentralization gave greater discretion to regional staff in development choices than ever before in any independent country in Eastern Africa, and emphasized the management role of the development directors in leading their teams of specialist officers; but it was far too early for any evaluation of the system to be possible.

The most disappointing experience has been in the formulation and implementation of development plans for particular areas (see Chambers 1973 for Kenya and Tanzania). The most common outcome has been plan formulation without implementation (See also pp. 139—46.). This has taken three main forms. The first, the disaggregation of national targets to local levels as an incentive to staff, cannot properly be called area management, since the staff were not involved in setting the targets, the targets were often unrealistic, and the attempt an outright failure. The second form was the preparation of long shopping lists of projects, justified by the needs for "participation" in planning, compiled with enthusiasm and in considerable detail by local-level staff and sent in to Ministries of Planning for incorporation in the national plan. This occurred as a preliminary to the second plans of Kenya, Tanzania and Zambia, but in each case the large stacks of local proposals were regarded with despair by central economists and largely ignored in the formulation of the national plan. The third form of planning without implementation has been data collection without the preparation of practicable action proposals, typically carried out by high-powered teams from the centre who leave behind a so-called "plan" for an area which joins the other unused and unusable documents on the shelves of government offices. The outcomes of these various failures are not just that nothing happens; they involve costs in

19

the time of government staff, in government expenditure, and most seriously of all, in the disillusion of local-level staff who become realistically cynical about any further attempt at area planning.

Area planning with implementation has been rare. The most important example is probably the Special Rural Development Programme (SRDP) in Kenya. Since this has provided much of the experience on which subsequent discussion is based, its history can be briefly outlined (see also Nellis 1972a; Gerhart 1971). Its origin can be traced back to the widespread concern with the school-leaver problem in the mid-1960's. This led to a joint University of Nairobi and Kenya Government conference on education, employment and rural development held at Kericho in 1966 (for the papers of which see Sheffield ed. 1967). This was followed by a report by a university team, by the appointment of an adviser to the Ministry of Economic Planning and Development to follow-up on the conference, and in 1968 by a joint government and university survey of fourteen rural divisions in Kenya chosen to represent a range of conditions of population density, development potential, and degree of development (see Hayer, Ireri and Moris 1971, for a description of the survey and its findings). Six of the fourteen areas were chosen for a first phase and in 1969 and early 1970 plans were prepared for five of them through a combination of ideas and effort from divisional, district, and provincial and headquarters staff. One of the "plans" prepared largely by a French technical assistance team was almost unusable but an area programme was salvaged through headquarters contributions, while another "plan" was so poor that it was deferred. Five plans were submitted in the form of a first year's budget for 1970/71 but the Treasury allocated only token votes, and implementation was delayed for six months while the estimates were further justified to the Treasury. In 1971 the programme then got off to a late start. Administrative officers, known as Area Coordinators, were posted to each of the first phase divisions and made responsible for co-ordinating all development under the SRDP, for overcoming bottlenecks, and for assisting departmental officers. Some plans for second phase areas were prepared but then shelved as it became clear that with the few SRDP headquarters staff in the Ministry of Economic Planning and Development (varying between one and three officers) it would be a major effort simply to service and develop the programmes in the six first phase areas. In early 1973 the future of the SRDP looked uncertain, despite many important achievements. For several months the adviser who had

20

pioneered and entrepreneured the SRDP had been managing what had become a complex and many-faceted programme virtually single-handed and on his departure the headquarters staff were not increased.

The objectives of the programme were frequently stated as being to raise rural incomes, to increase rural employment opportunities, to work through and sharpen the existing machinery of government, and to test experimental projects which after evaluation might be replicated on a wider scale. Technical assistance inputs from the donors which supported five of the areas[1] were kept low in order to maintain the goal of replicability. The experimental objective was important, but proved more difficult to achieve than expected because of the amount of imagination, time and effort required to devise, test and evaluate an experiment. It did, however, provide opportunities for the development of some of the management systems which are described in chapters 2 and 3, and also generated the experience on which parts of other chapters are based.

The SRDP demonstrated, as did the earlier experiences with target disaggregation, shopping lists, and data plans, the extreme difficulties of area planning without decentralization. It went further and exposed many of the problems of implementation, particularly the delays in fund releases which so often hold up and sometimes destroy projects in the field. It also showed, despite able management at the centre and good inter-ministerial cooperation, that the main bottleneck in rural development in Kenya was in Nairobi, just as in Zambia it was in Lusaka, and in Tanzania it was in Dar es Salaam at least until the bold decentralization of 1972.

*

Taken as a whole, the experience with government-administered initiatives in rural development in the countries of Eastern Africa up until the early 1970's fell far short of what had been needed and hoped for. The enthusiasm for multi-sector bounded-site programmes and projects which followed independence waned as their multiple diffi-

[1] The five areas and their donor support were: Kapenguria in Rift Valley Province—Holland; Kwale in Coast Province—ODA (Britain); Mbere in Eastern Province—NORAD (Norway); Migori in Nyanza Province—SIDA (Sweden) at first with FAO; and Vihiga in Western Province—USAID. The sixth area, Tetu in Central Province, was supported by the Kenya Government.

culties, their limited impact, and sometimes the dominance of foreigners in their management became evident. Except in Tanzania where the *ujamaa* programme received high and widespread priority, they were properly regarded more as potentially useful bonuses in rural development than as major cornerstones of strategy. Instead, attention turned to sectoral programmes and area management and to the more complex and intractable problems of mobilizing the huge government field administrations for more effective action in those rural areas where the vast majority of the population lived. It became more important than ever to analyze past shortcomings and to see how they might be surmounted in the future.

3. Four diagnoses and a missing prescription

Four diagnoses were popular in the 1960's and continue to receive support: they attribute shortcomings to lack of high-level manpower; to poor attitudes among public servants; to lack of integration and co-ordination; and to inappropriate structures. All have some validity; but each one can generate misleading recommendations for remedial action because of a vital missing prescription.

In the first place, shortage of high-level manpower was quite obviously a serious constraint in all the countries of Eastern Africa in the 1960's, and it remains serious in some, such as Botswana, in the early 1970's. De-Europeanizing and Africanizing an administration, undertaking additional functions including defence, foreign affairs and closer management of the economy, creating and staffing parastatals, Africanizing the private sector—from the time of independence onwards these tasks created a demand for high-level manpower which far exceeded the supply. The manpower planning of the 1960's had a crucial part to play in mitigating the crisis and in identifying ways in which it could be overcome. Too often, however, "a lack of high-level manpower" was used as an excuse for poor performance and for failing to probe into its causes, and as a polite expression to cover up culpable inefficiency and corruption. It was a convenient explanation: it placed blame correctly on the failure of the colonial administration to develop education and training faster, but in so doing it distracted attention from ways of improving performance. Moreover, manpower planning suited the economists who dominated planning ministries since it required a numerate approach and was something they could do. It made a contribution to national development and to localizing the public service and the private sector and will no doubt continue to do so. But by the early 1970's lack of high-level manpower had lost much of its explanatory power in evaluating the performance of field administration. In most of the countries of Eastern Africa the great majority of field staff were qualified nationals, many with substantial experience. Technical assistance personnel tended to be concentrated in the capital. There were indeed shortages of manpower in certain specialist fields like road engineering or water development, exacerbated by the heavy demands for the rural services they could provide. But in general, in rural field administration, high-level local qualified staff were in post. The issue had become much less one of numbers of trained staff, and much more one of their performance and output on the job.

Superficially, this supports the second diagnosis, that field staff are poorly motivated, lack entrepreneurial attitudes, drink too much, work too little, and spend too much time on their private interests. Again, it is a convenient explanation. For those who work in the capital it shifts responsibility to the field. It can also be made plausible through citing the individual examples of lack of initiative, alcoholism, or neglect of work which can be found in any large organization. Often, however, an examination of the work environment, perceptions and expectations of field staff will show, not that they are wilfully negligent, but that they are reacting rationally to a situation in which it is not clear what is expected of them but in which it *is* clear that the exercise of initiative in development matters is at least as likely to be penalized as deviant behaviour as rewarded for being good work. If this picture appears overdrawn, the reader should think himself into a field staff member's view of the world. At its most pathological his work life is liable to consist of sudden transfers (leading to acute problems of family separation and continuity in children's education), of sudden changes in those staff immediately senior to him, in a flow of mutually incompatible instructions and programmes from head-quarters, overlaying and eventually burying one another, in demands for information which is never used or for plans which are never acted on (or if acted on, are not implemented while he is still in the post), in high-powered flying visits by senior officers in which snap decisions are taken and instructions issued on the basis of patently inadequate information, in alternations between periods of being ignored and periods of intense but superficial evaluation. It is, of course, difficult to generalize between levels in organizations, between different organizations, and between countries. Nevertheless much of the poor performance of field staff can be attributed to their work situation, and it seems fair to suggest that if they had better projects to implement, were better and more consistently supervised, had greater continuity of service in one place, were more involved in planning their own work, and were evaluated and rewarded by results, in short, if management were better, their performance would improve sharply.

A third misleading diagnosis is a lack of integration and co-ordination. "Integrated" rural development became very popular in international circles in the latter 1960's. The origins of this usage would make a fascinating subject for research. One of the sources was the peculiar and pressing need for specialized agencies of the United Nations to reduce rivalry and to work better together. "Integrated" development meant development in which several UN agencies collaborated, or were meant to collaborate. Much loose thought and many vacuous statements were permitted, encouraged and made temporarily respectable by the vogue of integration. It is perhaps a little unfair to chastise the authors of UN documents, since desperate mental gymnastics may be needed in order to achieve the compromises which make their issue possible at all; but a quotation from the UN publication *Integrated Approach to Rural Development in Africa* will illustrate the obscure generality which sometimes resulted:

... the concept of the "integrated" approach in the context of rural development means an "integral" approach in the sense that it is a highly structural and systematic exercise in which all components in the system of development can be understood as important and appreciated for the part which they play individually and collectively. In this sense, the concept differs from the "harmonization" of plans and the "co-operation" of various agencies. It also has significance for the co-ordination of rural development plans.

(UN 1971:42)

Whatever meaning statements like this may have they scarcely help in trying to see how to get things done.

Equally, the word "co-ordination" provides a handy means for avoiding responsibility for clear proposals. It is perhaps for this reason that it is much favoured by visiting missions who are able to conceal their ignorance of how an administrative system works or what might be done about it by identifying "a need for better co-ordination". Indeed, a further research project of interest would be to test the hypothesis that the value of reports varies inversely with the frequency with which the word "co-ordination" is used. Moreover, by using "integrated" and "co-ordinated" more or less synonymously and in alternate sentences, long sections of prose can be given an appearance of saying something while in fact saying very little indeed.

When the activities to which they refer are looked at in detail "integration" and "co-ordination" can be seen to have heavy costs as well as benefits. The integrated approach to rural development is liable to mean a simultaneous implementation of many different programmes in the same area. But if rural development is seen as a sequence, then programmes themselves should follow sequences. Further, an attack on many fronts in one area may involve a wasteful and inequitable concentration of resources. Integration and co-ordination are too easily regarded as automatic benefits. If integration and co-ordination are good, the thinking goes, then maximum integration and maximum co-ordination are best of all. But unless interaction between officials is regarded as an end in itself, this is patently untrue. Co-ordination can have high costs in staff time spent in meetings and in dealing with paperwork. With maximum co-ordination staff time would be completely taken up in meetings and arrangements and the output would be nil. Co-ordination and integration should in fact be optimised, not maximised. Unconnected projects are best implemented in an unconnected fashion. And even when projects are connected, the costs as well as the benefits or whatever procedures are proposed for relating them together have to be weighed in assessing whether they would better continue independently.

These two words have done grave disservice by allowing vague thinking and by discouraging identification in detail of certain important relationships and potential benefits. The processes of rural development may be helped through organizing the activities of government and other agencies so that they complement one another, do not duplicate one another, do not compete for the same resources, and use scarce resources sparingly. In some rural development programmes and projects more than others, it may be worthwhile to arrange collaboration between agencies, joint planning of programmes, programming the sequence and timing of activities, sharing transport, addressing the same meetings, and so on. For example, projects for women's groups, including vegetable-growing, nutrition, health, family planning, and home economics may involve several departments: there may be substantial benefits from joint planning of the work to avoiding overlapping and to avoid confusing or overloading the groups. Sequences of extension work may also be planned. But making proposals in this sort of detail is often uncongenial and difficult for consultants, advisers and civil servants. It is tempting and easy to take refuge in statements like ". . . there should be better co-ordination between departments X and Y in order to achieve an integrated approach to Z", instead of thinking the problem through and saying something like "a meeting should be held at the end of each month, chaired by A, attended by B and C, at which joint work programmes should be drawn up . . .", specifying the detail of the procedure.

A fourth common diagnosis is that there is something wrong with the structure of government. Recommendations flowing from this diagnosis can take several forms. One is the setting up of new organizations, usually parastatals. While there may be good reasons for such action, the costs are likely to be high—in new overheads, in staff transfers, in prolonging reliance on foreign personnel whether in the new organizations or in the organizations from which local staff are transferred, and in the energies devoted to creating the organization, overcoming its teething troubles, and establishing its position in the community of other organizations. But weighing against recognition of these costs is the ease with which a new organization can be recommended by a commission, committee, or adviser, and its attractiveness to civil servants for whom it often provides an opportunity for advancement. Another recommendation is that ministerial responsibilities should be realigned, with the transfer of departments (Community Development and Water Affairs being favourites) from one ministry to another. When the dust has settled, however, the staff of the department are usually to be found sitting at the same desks in the same offices doing the same work. The appearance of change on paper is not matched by a change in working realities. Yet another line of recommendation is for internal reorganization of departments, ministries, or government as a whole. This is more difficult to devise and more difficult to effect. The Tanzanian and Zambia decentralizations are examples of this approach. They demonstrate the detailed and imaginative thinking that is required, and the steady will that is needed for implementation. There can be little doubt that reforms like these can be amply justified and well worth the effort they require. But they too have costs. There is always a danger that they and other structural changes will divert attention from the less dramatic but sometimes more important task of making function more effectively those structures which already exist.

The analysis of these four diagnoses points to a missing prescription: improving management procedures. For high-level manpower and other staff in field situations, management procedures provide a point of entry for trying to improve performance through modifying the rules and practices which prevail in their working environments. Whatever integration and co-ordination are desirable can be promoted through careful procedural design; and procedures present an opportunity to improve the operation of existing government organizations as an alternative or complement to major structural change.

In practice, however, management procedures receive much less notice and care than they deserve. To academics they are often an unopened book and believed to be a very dull and unacademic one at that. To short-term consultants they are unattractive because procedural recommendations involve hard work and require a detailed understanding of the administrative system. To lower-level staff they are often empty rituals performed to placate their superiors. To senior government servants embroiled in day-to-day affairs they are just one extra burden, and are thought out under pressure, embodied in circulars, and then introduced on a national scale without either pretesting or subsequent evaluation. But the principles of experimental testing which apply to pilot projects should also apply to procedures. That this so rarely happens is one reason why the detailed rules and conventions by which government agencies in rural areas operate are so often crude and inappropriate, and why the better design of management procedures presents a key point of leverage for improving performance.

4. Shifts of focus

Further analysis of the experience with rural development plans, programmes and projects builds up a case for a series of shifts of focus and priority, with implications for future resource allocations, particularly of high-level manpower. There are four main thrusts.

First, urban bias is insidious and pervasive. All too often middle-

27

ranking civil servants in field postings intrigue and apply for transfers to the capital city. Those already in the capital only rarely make major field visits. Technical officers give de facto priority to urban projects to the neglect of rural. The financial allocations for towns are spent, while those for rural areas remain unspent. Rural development has to fight against a silent conspiracy of centripetal forces which amass human and material resources in the towns and cities. The main reasons are not far to seek. The most obvious is perhaps the educational systems which have oriented aspirations towards white collar jobs and the bright lights of the city. But for middle-ranking civil servants there is much more to it than that. They perceive, usually correctly, that status and chances of promotion vary inversely with distance from the capital: those working in central ministries have the best chances, while those who have disgraced themselves are sent to "penal" posts at the periphery. For technical officers such as water engineers, architects, roads engineers and electrical engineers, work in a city or town is likely to be more complex, more satisfying, and better professional experience than work in villages. Once installed in a central house and office, staff find it difficult to go out to rural areas even if they want to, and easy to stay if they do not. The round of official and domestic engagements, unexpected crises, sudden demands from the minister for a brief, and the number of people who may have to be consulted before a rural visit can be made, combine to chain the civil servant, often a happy prisoner, to his desk. But the application of financial and material resources requires personnel, and money is often spent where staff happen to reside. A major implication, understood in Tanzania and Zambia, is that, in order effectively to shift priorities to rural development, staff have themselves to be moved out into the rural areas.

Second, in rural development there has often been a failure to plan planning and plan management, both in headquarters and in the field. With some qualifications, desirable planning activities can be presented as a sequence:

(i)   plan formulation
(ii)   budgeting
(iii) programming
(iv) implementation
(v)   monitoring
(vi) evaluation *ex post*
(vii) reformulation of the plan
      (and repeat the sequence)

28

In practice, planners have concentrated on the first two activities to the neglect of the others: on plan formulation perhaps because of its intellectual attraction, its susceptibility to mathematical treatment, its insulation from the details of administration, and its position at the beginning of the sequence of activities; and on budgeting partly because of its undeniable priority and intractable deadlines. In line with these biases, planning literature has been preoccupied with plan formulation, presented as sets of procedures, with less detailed attention paid to implementation, presented as sets of problems. At both national and local levels, resources and effort have been devoted to data-collection, plan formulation and plan-writing, while programming, implementation, monitoring and evaluation have been relatively ignored. The common result— plan formulation without implementation— constitutes a form of mismanagement and misallocation of resources, but has been protected by the prestige of "planning" from the criticism it deserves.

Third, central planners, field administrators and politicians have been preoccupied with capital and development expenditure and with capital projects to the relative neglect of recurrent expenditure and of programmes which are implemented through existing field organizations. This preoccupation appears to have several origins. Donor agencies are biased towards financial aid tied to capital inputs. Economists can more easily carry out their professional activities with capital projects than with recurrent expenditure for which the data may be poor or non-existent. Field administrators find visible capital projects more satisfying, more creative, and easier to present as tangible evidence of development activity, than dispersed field programmes. Politicians, most particularly, need to be able to demonstrate achievements which their constituents will identify with their leadership. At the extreme, donor agencies (most notably the World Bank) may insist on the formation of a special agency to handle a programme or major project rather than working through and improving existing organizations.

From a national point of view, however, very large recurrent resources in the form of trained staff and operating expenses are already committed in the field. For some countries, the iceberg analogy is apposite: the visible tip represents the development projects which attract attention and analysis, while the larger recurrent commitments remain hidden and largely unanalyzed below. This phenomenon can be illustrated from the budgets of Kenya and Zambia.

	Percentage of total estimated government expenditure		Percentage of total estimated expenditure for Ministry of Agriculture	
	Capital	Recurrent	Capital	Recurrent
Kenya 1973/74	34	66	41	59
Zambia 1973	33	67	44	56

Sources: Republic of Kenya 1972a: 1 and 1972b: (ii)
Republic of Zambia 1973a: 4, 122—3, and 146. If the very heavy recurrent expenditure on agricultural subsidies in Zambia is included the percentages for the Ministry of Agriculture become capital—20 and recurrent—80.

By way of illustration, in 1973/74 the Department of Technical Services in the Kenya Government's Ministry of Agriculture had a staff of nearly 14,000, of whom some 6,300 were junior and senior staff, of whom in turn over 3,000 were Agricultural Assistants, Animal Health Assistants and Animal Husbandry Assistants. For personal emoluments alone, the estimate was for K£4.2 million or 38 per cent of the Ministry's estimated recurrent expenditure (Republic of Kenya 1972a: 37, 40—1). Such heavy allocations as these are committed more or less automatically year by year and without more than marginal choices at a planning level. In planning activities, recurrent resources have thus been relatively neglected and there is a strong case for subjecting recurrent allocations and their use to more stringent appraisal, evaluation and management.

One factor in the lack of attention to recurrent resource allocation and management is what Moris (1972: 115) calls the "centrist ideology" of planning and administration—the system of beliefs and attitudes which holds that initiative and control do and should reside primarily in the capital city, and outside the capital city higher rather than lower in the hierarchy. A corollary of this view is the belief that field staff are generally rather incompetent and idle, a belief which is unlikely to foster the exercise of the discretion and responsibility required from them if they are to perform well. Without a management system which allows, encourages and rewards the exercise of initiative and the performance of good work, it is scarcely surprising that field staff have often appeared to those in the centre to justify adverse comment. The centrist ideology in fact sustains the conditions which justify it. Over-centralization prevents the exercise of initiative at the lower levels, good performance passes unnoticed, and field staff come fatalistically to accept as a fact of life the flow of instructions and plans from above in the formulation of which they have not played any part and for the implementation of which they do not expect to receive any credit. The authoritarian style of the internal administration of some departments is in sharp conflict with accepted management practices, but preserved by low visibility and the lack of management advisory services in governments. There are, of course, incompetent, poorly trained, and just plain lazy staff. But on the basis of many subjective impressions, and also of the experimental work reported in Chapter 2 and 3, it appears that most field staff have far greater capability for managing their work than most of their superior officers assume. An imaginative management approach to the operation of field agencies might mobilize and exploit the great potential at present cramped and constrained by outdated administrative outlooks and practices, many of which are hangovers from the colonial past.

The four main shifts implied by these analyses—from urban bias to rural; from plan formulation and budgeting to programming, implementation and monitoring; from capital projects to recurrent resource management; and from hierarchical, authoritarian administration to more decentralized and democratic management of field staff —combine with the earlier argument for more attention to procedures to make a case for reallocations of manpower resources and for training and recruitment for new skills. The implications are that more high-level manpower time should be devoted to improving the operation of existing government organizations; that specialists in such fields as management, organization and methods, and organizational behaviour, should be recruited and trained, perhaps with a compensating decrease in numbers of economist-planners; and that in those countries which have not effectively decentralized, there may be good reasons for posting more high-level staff to the field and giving them more responsibility.

5. Clusters of procedures

In the light of these arguments the scope of this book can now be defined more clearly. We are not primarily concerned with multi-sector bounded-site projects. They often have well-defined management systems and procedures: the Mwea Irrigation Settlement in

Kenya is an outstanding example. These systems, however, are often technocratic, derived from technical imperatives in the nature of the project. Moreover, management is typically what Moris (1972:128) calls "hub-and-wheel", with considerable authority and discretion vested in a central figure. We are, rather, concerned with the less clear-cut situations which prevail in sectoral programmes and in the various forms of area management. It is partly because management in these situations, which often lack an interdepartmental hierarchical authority, is less visible and appears harder to improve that it has been so neglected in the past and is now a high priority.

We are also largely limited in this book to management procedures —rules and practices which govern behaviour. There is a vast field of management which includes much of the human relations school, T groups, sensitivity training and the like, with which we are not primarily concerned. This is not to imply that such approaches do not have value. It is, rather, to suggest that procedures are a better starting point, and that the experience gained and the needs revealed through devising and introducing procedures will lead naturally towards training in management skills and techniques. The dangers of isolated partial reforms are notorious (Molander 1972), but these dangers may apply at least as much to management training without procedural reform as to procedural reform without management training. The thrust of the argument is that procedures provide a neglected but key point of entry.

For the sake of analysis and presentation, procedures can be identified as clusters which hang together. In doing this, a systems analysis approach can be used, (Belshaw and Chambers 1973a esp. pp. 5—9) following the pioneering work of Kulp (1971) in this field. In practice this has not meant much more than drawing boxes for the clusters of procedures and joining them with arrowed lines to indicate actual, desirable or possible connections. This approach makes discussion easier and shows graphically what would otherwise take much prose to present. There is nothing sacrosanct about the particular titles, boxes and lines which are used here (see figure 1). They have, however, proved useful in analysing the SRDP experience and in developing procedures for the SRDP and may be of use as categories for further work.

One of the shortcomings of a systems approach using a diagram such as this is the danger that for intellectual satisfaction and completeness it will be considered desirable to "close the circle", that is to

32

make information flow along all the connecting lines. Each flow, however, has its costs in staff time, as well as any possible benefits. It cannot be emphasized too strongly that despite the connections in the diagram, many of the systems can be introduced independently, and the reader must not be misled into supposing that there is anything like an all-or-nothing package.

A further qualification is that it may often be necessary to associate some structural change with the introduction of procedures. Area Coordinators were an essential component of the programming and implementation system introduced in the Kenya SRDP. Any proposal to introduce procedures should be preceded by a careful appraisal of who should do what and of the levels in the hierarchy at which different activities should take place. Some practical issues in procedure design are considered in Chapter 6.

It has proved useful to think in terms of six clusters of procedures, each of which is susceptible to largely independent experimental treatment. These are:

Programming and implementation
Field staff management
Local participation
Evaluation
Rural research and development
Plan formulation

The sequence in which these are listed is deliberate and is also the sequence in the following four chapters. A more logical order might start with plan formulation, leading into programming and implementation. But it has been precisely the logic of starting with plan formulation that has generated the stacks of unimplemented and unimplementable plans which moulder, fade and feed termites on the shelves of offices throughout Eastern Africa. A book which began logically with plan formulation would be in grave danger of repeating the experience and never fighting free from the innumerable considerations, qualifications and ramifications of plan making. Instead of being about managing rural development, it would be about planning techniques which, if followed, might well impede rural development. Listing the clusters of activities in this unconventional order is part of a deliberate attempt to maintain a balance in the book as well as to divert some attention and resources from the fashionable activities of evaluation, research and plan formulation to the more difficult and less developed activities of programming, implementation, the management of field staff, and local participation. For all too often the neglect or mishandling of these latter activities have been serious hindrances. And their importance can be expected to increase as governments struggle to give priority to rural development and as they come closer to grips with the obstinate and persistent impediments to getting things done in rural areas.

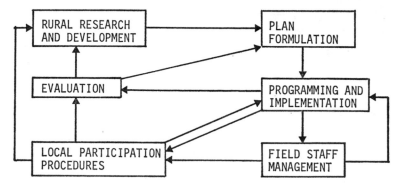

Figure I. *Clusters of procedures and some connections.*

(For a more detailed formulation, closer to an engineering systems presentation, see Belshaw and Chambers 1973a, figure I.)

II. What, Who, When and How: Programming and Implementation

If to do were as easy as to know what were good to do, chapels had been churches, and poor men's cottages princes' palaces

(Shakespeare, The Merchant of Venice)

Planners cannot limit themselves to saying *what* is to be achieved without showing *how* and by *whom* it is to be done.

(Waterston 1969:11)

1. Problems and opportunities

In Eastern Africa many of the difficulties which hinder the effective implementation of rural development programmes and projects can be traced to headquarters administration and policies in the capital cities. It is in the ministries of capital cities that locally-prepared plans have so often come to their final rest, that new programmes have been devised without field consultation or testing for feasibility, that unrealistic procedures have been worked out and promulgated and that fund releases have been delayed, so often destroying confidence and morale in the field. A Zambian Provincial Minister of State was speaking for field officers in many countries when he said:

Up to now ... I see nothing but confusion. Some heads of departments have no idea about what is supposed to be done. While some centralization is good, I think that after the plan has been accepted the decentralization will greatly facilitate the implementation of the plan. I am convinced that there are capable men and women in the provinces to carry out development projects. Why, for instance, should we wait for money for a good one year for a simple health centre, a small house for a court messenger, etc? Let money be released and let us in the provinces see to the building programme. The bottleneck in the four-year plan is Lusaka and if this tendency goes on what we intend to accomplish will be in the actual fact thrown into our faces.

(Hesse 1968 quoted by Tordoff 1968a:430 quoting the Minister of State for the Eastern Province)

In a similar vein, President Nyerere, introducing the proposals for decentralization in Tanzania, observed how projects put up from the field and involving several ministries at the centre might be prevented by any one of them, and went on to say:

But the most frequent complaint in the Districts and Regions is that they cannot get answers to their letters at all. They write and write, sometimes five times, and hear nothing, yet it is impossible for them to visit Dar es Salaam from a place like Sumbawanga, or even Morogoro, without permission—which they cannot get!

(Nyerere 1972)

The sense of impotence of field staff can be further illustrated by the remark of a District Governor in Zambia that the most that could happen at a district development committee was that a proposal could be forwarded to the province with the further request that "the Permanent Secretary ask his counterpart in Lusaka", to which he described as a typical reply "Those concerned are taking the matter up with those concerned" (Republic of Zambia 1972:90—1).

Both Tanzania and Zambia are attacking these impediments to action through radical decentralization. Structural change of this sort, especially when budgetary devolution is resolutely combined with posting staff out from the capital city and into the regions and provinces can unquestionably have a major part to play in improving implementation in the field. The arguments and emphases in this book are not in any sense directed against such an approach; on the contrary, one of the findings of the SRDP was that the main bottleneck in rural development was in Nairobi, that delayed fund releases in the centre were a frequent cause of failure in the field, and that without budgetary devolution this bottleneck would be difficult to overcome. But decentralization is a long-term process and proposals for structural change can all too easily divert attention from the immediate opportunities which lie to hand.

Whatever is done, procedures are required for implementation. If structural change is undertaken, new operating procedures have to be devised and introduced. If structural change is not undertaken, procedures are all the more important as a point of leverage for improving performance. In all the regions, provinces and districts of Eastern

Africa there are official programmes and projects already in the process of implementation by field staff. Whether there is structural
change or not, two key questions can without delay be asked about
these on-going initiatives at field level: what impedes implementation?,
and, how could implementation be improved?

Many responses could be given to the first question, but from the
experience gained with the SRDP and elsewhere in Eastern Africa,
seven problems appear especially prevalent and damaging at the lower
levels of rural management. In their more pathological forms these
are:

(i) *authoritarian management:* a senior officer issues orders, does
not listen to his subordinates' problems, and does not encourage initiative on their part. He feels insecure and defends and reassures himself through asserting his superior authority. His subordinates respond
with deference and a reluctance to present requests, and only report
information they think will be well received.

(ii) *wasteful meetings:* an excessive amount of staff time is taken
up with meetings. Staff sit through long sessions when only a small
part, if any, of the business concerns them. Meetings are either talking
shops which do not lead to decisions or action, or captive audiences for
a senior officer whose decisions are not influenced by discussion.

(iii) *excessive reports:* Too many reports have to be compiled. Too
much information is required in the reports. The information takes too
long to collect or invent, and would be misleading if it were ever
made use of, which it is not. Additional reports are required, and additional information is required in existing reports, but reports are rarely
stopped and information requirements rarely reduced.

(iv) *departmentalism:* staff of different departments compete rather
than collaborate, regard one another as rivals, and work independently
of one another when they should co-operate. The results are conflicts,
confusion, duplication and gaps, all hindering the progress of development programmes.

(v) *top-down targetry:* work targets are decided at a high level and
then disaggregated down the hierarchy. Local-level staff take no part
in setting their own targets. The targets they are given are either too
high or too low or are meaningless since their achievement depends on
influences (such as the weather, prices, or farmer choices) which are
outside their control.

(vi) *inadequate resources:* staff lack the resources they need, such
as housing, transport, funds for petrol, materials, or agricultural in-

puts, and they also lack any means whereby they can communicate their needs and the costs of their not being met to those who allocate the resources in question.

(vii) *ineffective work programming:* monthly work programmes are sometimes drawn up but are subject to many changes. Projects are not programmed and reports do not indicate progress with projects in any systematic manner.

Looked at another way, these and other problems at the field level can be seen as opportunities; for if they can be mitigated or overcome, implementation should improve. There are, no doubt, a great many ways in which they can be tackled. In describing any one experience, there are obvious dangers of focusing attention on some methods to the neglect of others. The justification for outlining the particular approach developed at one stage of the Kenya SRDP is not that it provides comprehensive solutions, nor even that it is necessarily replicable; and certainly not that it presents a finished or final system. It is rather that the experience and details may be of value to others who also try to improve rural management through new procedures and may help them to devise better and probably simpler systems. It may also help them to avoid some of the mistakes we made. After the event it is tempting to rationalize the original purpose of the system and relate them to what in practice it seemed to achieve. In fact, however, the path was far from straight and new needs and problems were perceived as work proceeded.

2. Developing the system

It was only gradually that it became evident that a full procedural system for programming and implementation was needed for the Kenya SRDP.[1] The process began in 1970 when it became policy that an administrative officer of the Provincial Administration, to be known as an Area Co-ordinator, would be posted to each of the six SRDP divisions (sub-districts). In summary, his functions were officially described as:

● to help officers at all levels to get the programme started, and in particular to tackle problems as they arose at the different levels, not

1. For a brief description of the SRDP, see pages 20—21.

attempting to dictate to other departments, but acting in a support role;
- to act as a communications link between divisional, district and provincial levels and interministerially between departments, speeding up the communication of information;
- to act as a contact or link man with donor representatives, evaluators and visitors;
- to draw up timetables and work programmes to maintain the momentum of the programme.

In practice, Area Co-ordinators found themselves thrust into a job for which there were no precedents and in which much was left to their initiative. They were in an awkward position: on the one hand expected to "co-ordinate" and to push through the implementation of projects, but on the other lacking any formal authority over their peers in other departments.

At this time a commission (the Ndegwa Commission) was reviewing the efficiency of the public service in Kenya and its subsequent report (Republic of Kenya 1971a) pointed to the connection between past failures in rural planning and poor or non-existent procedures. It attributed the difficulties of development committees, for example, partly to the lack of definition of the "actual duties and responsibilities of all the members of these committees, and the routines to be followed in plan-implementation, progress-reporting and plan revision at the District level" (Republic of Kenya 1971a:115). The need of Area Co-ordinators for detailed guidelines fitted in with this new priority concern, and the experimental environment provided by the SRDP presented a timely opportunity for social scientists to innovate and learn the hard way in testing ideas in this largely unexplored area. Lying as it did somewhere between the applied social sciences, public administration, management, and Organization and Methods, it was no man's land which we entered with some uncertainty.

Interestingly, the first main need perceived for Area Co-ordinators was not a comprehensive management system, but procedures and layout for reporting. In response to a request to devise such procedures, we thought that four sets of points should be borne in mind when framing a reporting system:

(i) Report-writing should not be a substitute for other action. Reports take time to write, may be delayed through time-lags in information becoming available, and are sometimes held up in typing, duplicating, and in the post. Urgent issues must always be dealt with immediately, usually by telephone, telegram or word of mouth and not reserved for a report.

(ii) Restraint should be exercised in requests for information. An intellectually perfectionist approach to management control requires the obtaining and communication of a great deal of information, but this has its costs. Lower-level staff find report-writing a great chore and their time has an opportunity cost. Also, most of the information in most reports is never used.

(iii) Care should be exercised not to ask for information which, though apparently desirable, would be misleading because of its probable inaccuracy.

(iv) Area Co-ordinators' reports should be designed with the following purposes in mind:

- developing their roles and relationships;
- improving and maintaining staff and programme performance;
- securing necessary action at the various levels of government;
- recording progress for continuing and subsequent evaluation;
- forcing staff into continual self-evaluation and feedback;
- developing and maintaining commitment to the programme;
- developing the planning and replanning process;
- identifying problems and bottlenecks and securing action to overcome them;
- improving the government's existing reporting systems.

This last set of points took us far beyond the confines of a mere reporting system. What had happened was that, forced to ask the purpose of reporting, we were confronted with the ritual irrelevance of the great mass of existing government reports, the bulk of which were devoted to routine observations and statistics unrelated to on-going projects or the problems which they faced. We decided to try to follow the principle that reports should be functional, and that a clear benefit should be identified with each category of information included in them. This drove us into realizing that the reports would have to be oriented to problems, opportunities and action. Further, in reporting on progress, one purpose would be to identify lags in implementation and to secure remedial action. But this in turn required that operations should have been programmed, so that performance could be assessed against what had been planned. Also, a potential use of reports was to provide data for evaluation by recording progress and

40

problems, so that future planning and programming could be improved. We were, thus, forced by the principle that reports should be functional into developing backward linkages to the programming of operations and forward linkages to operation control and evaluation. We moved from reporting into a management system. The objectives became to work out, test and improve procedures to enable Area Coordinators to develop their roles and carry out their functions; and to develop those procedures into a management system for rural development programmes and projects which might perhaps be of use more widely within Kenya and elsewhere.

We recognized some of the dangers of systems for programming and controlling the implementation of rural development programmes and projects (Belshaw and Chambers, 1971). Excessive or unnecessary information might be demanded. Unreliable and misleading information might be generated by demanding quantification of achievements upon which reporting staff thought they would be judged. Programmes, or the balance between programmes, might be biased, as in the rural development programme in Malaysia (Ness 1967:124—141), towards construction projects because construction was easily quantified and inspected. Staff might be demoralized through the setting from above of unattainable targets. Self-help and participation by the people might become forced rather than voluntary if officials were required to achieve self-help targets in their areas. In designing the system we tried to avoid these traps and where possible to improve on previous practice; but as we found, it is far, far easier to be aware of these pitfalls than effectively to avoid them.

We drew eclectically on several sources of ideas. We considered the critical path method but rejected it as too complex for use at the field level. While good for a complicated project such as a major construction work, setting up a factory, or even a land settlement scheme (as illustrated by Millikan 1967), especially when there are inexorable deadlines (as Butcher (1971) has shown where a population is being displaced by a lake forming behind a dam), a critical path method is less useful for simpler projects and programmes. Those engaged on the implementation of low-level rural development programmes are normally well aware of the linkages between activities and can carry them in their heads without recourse to any representation as complex as a network diagram. Moreover, although the critical path method had been taught in public administration courses, we knew of no case where it had ever been used in a low-level rural development field

41

situation. In spite of these reservations, however, we did find the first stage of network analysis to be useful—identifying and listing the operations to be carried out, and this was incorporated as one component of the system.

There were also other sources of ideas. We adopted some features of a bar chart monitoring system, updated through monthly reports, that was in use in the Ministry of Works in Nairobi. Some of the principles of Management by Objectives (MBO) (Humble 1967; Garrett and Walker 1969; Reddin 1971) were also used, especially the precept that performance targets should not be set from above by a supervisor, but by the subordinate himself in discussion with his supervisor. Another practice that was incorporated was the technique of using a blackboard to write up participants' ideas and to focus discussion, borrowed from case study teaching methods. Yet another source was the Malaysian operations room and red book system (Ferguson 1965; Ness 1967; Kulp 1970:633—651). The complete system seemed too mechanistic and did not appear adequately to pinpoint bottlenecks in the course of implementation, but the practices of keeping visible records of progress and of holding regular progress reviews were accepted.

The system for managing programming and implementation which we put together from these and other sources was thoroughly discussed with those who were to use it. This was a most important stage. Headquarters staff, Provincial Planning Officers and Area Co-ordinators themselves suggested a number of modifications which were adopted. The pilot system was finally agreed at a meeting attended by field staff held at the Kenya Institute of Administration in July 1971 and was then implemented for the 1971/72 financial year in four of the six SRDP areas. Headquarters staff attended the first programming meetings in the field. In the course of these, procedures were improvised and adapted, and techniques developed in one area were transferred to others. After a year's operation of the system, discussions were held with Provincial Planning Officers and Area Co-ordinators and some further changes were made. In 1972, however, the main system operated without assistance from research staff and continued thereafter in all six areas without a further research and development input. In 1973 there was some decline in support from headquarters, but at the same time some simplifications were introduced. For a time a weakness of the system had been that partly because care had been taken to serve the needs of field staff, senior headquarters staff had been less involved; and one major lesson from the experience is the importance of support at the senior civil servant or higher political level for research and development work on management procedures.

There is nothing sacrosanct about the details of the system. In any other context, modifications will be desirable. In devising a management system for another administrative environment, it may be more important to appreciate and use the experience gained with this system and the principles which are embedded in it than to adopt particular procedural details. But to appreciate these and how they affect implementation, the framework of the system must first be outlined.

3. The programming and implementation management (PIM) system

The PIM system is difficult to describe because from 1971 onwards it was continually changing and actual practice sometimes diverged from instruction and theory. We were deliberately permissive in this since we felt it was important that staff in the field should be able to modify details to suit their needs as they perceived them. The description which follows puts together parts of the system all of which were used and all of which, to the best of our judgement, were useful in the SRDP context and may be useful elsewhere.

The full PIM system has three main components:

a *programming exercise*, which in the SRDP was annual and held just before or just after the beginning of the financial year. This is a meeting attended by all those directly concerned with implementation at which they jointly and freely draw up a phased work programme for the year;

a *management meeting*, which in the SRDP was usually monthly. At this meeting attended by those concerned directly with implementation, progress is reviewed against the phased work programme, bottlenecks are identified, and remedial action agreed upon;

an *action report* which in the SRDP was described as a monthly management report, summarizing briefly the progress made and problems encountered, naming those responsible for action, and sent quickly and simultaneously to those concerned at different levels in government.

To make this system work, an action co-ordinator (in the SRDP the Area Co-ordinator) is needed to call together staff for the programming exercise and the management meetings and to write and distribute the action reports. (For more detailed and SRDP-specific description of the system see appendix pages 176—198.)

(i) The Programming Exercise

The programming exercise is the most crucial part of the system. For any given project, programming involves agreeing what has to be done, who is responsible for doing it, and when each operation should start and finish. Only when this has been done can the management meetings and action reports follow on.

The first decision is which projects should be programmed. In the SRDP the system was used for a very wide range of projects including crop extension programmes, farm credit, fertilizer demonstrations, dairy development, dips, farmer training, a farm management experiment, young farmers' clubs, home economics, crop trials and research, a ranch, road construction, water supplies, vector control, health centre construction, housing, a mobile health clinic, women's clubs, day care centres, self-help development, land adjudication, roads and co-operative development. If a large number of projects are programmed, however, the system becomes overloaded and burdensome. In general, those projects should be preferred which have higher national priority, involve larger resources, and require the collaboration of larger numbers of departments and levels within hierarchies.

For each project in turn the action co-ordinator invites those staff members directly concerned with implementation to a joint programming meeting which is held either just before or just after the start of the financial year. The person from headquarters who is responsible for the necessary fund releases also attends. Those present may be from one or more ministries and departments, and from one or more levels in the hierarchy. It is important that all the officers responsible for implementation should take part and the action co-ordinator has to ensure that they all speak their minds freely, contribute from their experience, and raise objections where appropriate, without fear of any senior officer who may be present.

Discussion starts with an open-minded examination of the objectives of the project. These may not be clear and the value of the project may be questioned. In such cases, follow-up action may be decided and the meeting adjourned. As and when there is agreement on objectives, their desirability, and the potential of the project for achieving

44

them, the programming exercise can begin.

The main stages of programming are:

1. listing and agreeing the operations to be carried out;
2. identifying and agreeing who is responsible for each operation;
3. agreeing start and completion times for each operation;
4. agreeing targets and a completion indicator for each operation;
5. checking for feasibility, agreement, and acceptance of targets.

Three techniques are useful in varying combinations. First, a large blackboard can be used for listing the operations involved, who is responsible, the duration of each operation, and the completion indicators. The action co-ordinator makes entries on the board as suggested by the participants. This technique has much to recommend it. It is flexible; entries can be rubbed out or added in; rough working is easy; and most important of all, the participants can all see what is being agreed and are all discussing the same visible information and proposals, allowing only slight possibilities of misunderstanding. A second technique is for each participant to have a phasing form (appendix D) on which he enters the same information. This, however, does not show the relationships between the timings of operations as clearly as a bar chart. A third technique is for each participant to have a programming chart (appendix E) which incorporates the same information as on the blackboard. Different people prefer different combinations of these three devices. Any approach which does not use a blackboard is liable to misunderstandings between participants, and some who are less familiar with the system may get left behind by the discussion and even be unaware of what they are believed to be agreeing to. The recommended combination is a blackboard and a programming chart. In this combination, once the details have all been agreed, each participant copies them off the board onto a chart, and takes that away as a record of what has been agreed in the meeting.

Using the blackboard, the sequence is as follows. The component operations of the project are listed vertically on the left hand side in rough chronological order. Participants identify operations which have been forgotten. When the list is complete and agreed, those responsible for implementation are identified and listed in the next column. The months are written across the board and any inexorable deadlines (for example, connected with crop seasons) are marked in under them. The timings of any operations which cannot be completed before a certain date (for instance, using a standard lead time for fund releases) are then entered. Through informal discussion, bars are then drawn in to indicate the timings and duration of all the operations. Where possible and appropriate, quantified targets are discussed and agreed and written in at the ends of months. Completion indicators—the events or outputs which will show that the operations have been completed—are entered on the right hand side for each operation.

There is then a very important stage: a thorough, openminded and non-authoritarian checking of the feasibility of the implementation proposals as presented on the board. It is at this stage that the action co-ordinator can encourage participating staff to think carefully about the "how" of implementation, about the resources which will be needed, the timing of their supply, their adequacy for the tasks and targets proposed, and the most likely hitches that may arise. Possible snags and bottlenecks are discussed and remedial action considered. Through this open questioning and testing for feasibility the action co-ordinator tries to ensure that the proposals are realistic and that all those responsible for execution are fully and freely committed to the programme and to achieving their part in it.

Finally, each participant copies out the operations, who is responsible, timings, completion indicators, and other details onto programming charts or phasing forms and takes them away as a record of what he and others have agreed to do and as a guide for action.

(ii) The Management Meeting

After the programming exercise, regular meetings are held between the action co-ordinator and those responsible for implementation at the local level. The frequency of these meetings depends on circumstances. Monthly may be near optimal for many programmes: more frequent meetings might take excessive amounts of staff time; wider intervals might allow slippage in operations to get out of hand without remedial action. Attendance is limited to those concerned with implementation.

At the meeting the action co-ordinator checks through the programming charts and asks about all operations which should be in hand, which should have been completed, or which are due to start in the coming month. The officers responsible report on progress and problems. The programming charts are then entered in green for on time or on target and red for behind time or below target. Remedial action is discussed and decided.

(iii) The Action Report

The word "report" is misleading since this is an operational control device for securing action, not a means for communicating routine information. The report follows directly on from the management meeting, the findings of which it records. It is written by the action co-ordinator soon after the meeting and distributed quickly and widely.

The report has two main sections. The first is a short sharp statement of the position and of action required, based on the programming chart: for each project it lists the operations which are or should be active, the target for the month's end, the actual achievement, whether (YES or NO) the operation is on time, the remedial action required if it is not on time, and who should take that action. The persons from whom action is requested have their initials circled in red on the copies they receive so that they focus quickly and do not have to read the whole document. The second section of the report is also brief, but elaborates on what has happened and specifies more exactly what needs to be done and the implications of delay.

In the SRDP the report was unusual in being sent simultaneously to different departments and to the different levels in government that were involved, including ministry headquarters, province, district, sub-district and below. The normal lengthy process of feeding upwards through layers in the hierarchy was thus avoided, though intermediate levels were kept informed.

Obviously, various formats for the action report are possible. What is most important is that the action required and who should take it are clearly identified and that this is communicated quickly. Delays in issuing the report seriously reduce its value. The SRDP experience suggests that for the sake of brevity and effect the report should not be used for all the rural development projects in an area, but only for those which are of higher priority. The particular format used in the SRDP (see appendix F) was linked with the programming chart. The entries of YES or NO in the "On Time" column enabled recipients to enter up their programming charts which then presented a visual record of implementation throughout the year.

The result enables operations rooms to be maintained with charts displayed so that the state of implementation of the projects can be seen at a glance. As with so many devices of this sort, unless there is constant attention this part of the system can fall behind. It is desirable to routinize the making of entries on the charts, a task for which executive or clerical staff can be trained. The charts in the operations rooms then simplify briefings, and enable a quick appreciation of targets, achievements, and bottlenecks.

4. An evaluation of the PIM approach

The PIM approach as developed in the SRDP has been the subject of four evaluations (Nellis 1972 b; IDS 1972; Belshaw and Chambers 1973b; and Chabala, Kiiru, Mukuna and Leonard 1973). In addition it was reviewed and modified by Area Co-ordinators and Provincial Planning Officers in periodical meetings from 1971 through 1973. The evaluations were generally favourable and criticisms led in some cases to improvements and simplifications in the system. In attempting an evaluation here I am vulnerable to personal bias, with the twin dangers of being overly favourable or of falling over backwards and being hypercritical. While I am unlikely fully to succeed, I try in what follows to tread a middle course.

In any evaluation it is important to take into account the particular circumstances of the SRDP. On the one hand, the experimental rationale and the need of Area Co-ordinators to legitimate themselves and their roles probably made it unusually easy to gain initial acceptance of the system from field staff without a high degree of authoritative commitment from the upper levels of government: as usual, it was fairly easy to make a pilot project "succeed". On the other hand, this lack of high-level authoritative commitment meant that following staff changes in 1973 the support needed in the centre for the system to function was in doubt. For these reasons no evaluation should therefore be unduly influenced either by the easy initial acceptance of the system or by any subsequent decline in its operation.

It must also be stressed that the procedures and forms in the appendices are not put forward as a model to be copied. They represent a stage, and a far from perfect stage, in the development of a system. The reader who has the patience to understand them may quickly see possible improvements such as amalgamating the phasing forms (appendix D) and programming charts (appendix E), or modifying the report (appendix F) so that all the information on a project is presented on one sheet instead of in two places. The procedures and forms are presented here only to enable the reader to go deeper into the system if

48

he wishes. Since they may appear confusing at first sight, it is worth pointing out that the initial reaction of most evaluators was that the system was overelaborate but that they changed this view once they came to understand it and to appreciate that the staff who were using it were well able to make it work.

We can start evaluation by considering the system in relation to the seven problems of the lower levels of rural management which were listed earlier (pages 37—38):

(i) *authoritarian management.* The system introduces and the procedures require a more democratic, egalitarian and less hierarchical managerial style than is usually found in field administration in Eastern Africa. To be effective, joint programming demands the contributions and free assent of participants, not only from different departments but also from different levels in the same department. In the group meeting authoritarian relationships tend to break down. In the SRDP subordinate officers sometimes found it much easier to communicate their difficulties and needs to their superiors in programming meetings than in other situations. Further, where there was an authoritarian technical senior officer, the Area Co-ordinator was sometimes able to act as a sort of therapist through careful questioning and through encouraging subordinates to make their views known. The action report also treated all those responsible for implementation equally in that action could be requested by the relatively low level of the Division from higher levels in the hierarchy, and also exposed to all its recipients whatever bottlenecks and delinquencies there might have been at those higher levels. As Chabala and others (1973:8—9) pointed out, the PIM system reversed the flow of demands along the hierarchy so that subordinates could make demands of their superiors, putting pressure on them to provide whatever assistance they needed in order to improve their productivity.

(ii) *wasteful meetings.* Meetings which are general talking shops have no place in the system. The procedures for the programming exercise and for the management meetings are closely tied down to the details of implementation, of who should do what, when and how. SRDP meetings were, as a consequence, quite dramatically different from, for example, the early meetings of district development committees when their functions had not been clearly defined. The austere functional nature of the monthly meetings in the SRDP was most interestingly reflected in the numbers who attended. Who should be invited was initially left largely to the discretion of the Area Co-ordinators. Where a large number of participants were invited, the meetings were generally much less effective and the projects were less energetically implemented than where attendance was limited to those directly concerned with implementation. In 1972 some Area Co-ordinators went further and under pressure of time began to substitute short meetings with individual officers for the larger and more formal meetings, while still compiling the action reports on the basis of the information obtained.

(iii) *excessive reports*. Routine ritualistic reports describing the weather, visits, miscellaneous statistics and minor matters have no place in the system. The action report is problem- and opportunity-oriented, and designed not as a "report" but as a direct management tool for getting things done. As already described, reports very easily become excessively detailed, long, delayed, and ineffective. At one time the amount of information and reporting demanded of Area Co-ordinators in the SRDP was excessive and dysfunctional, though much of the load resulted not from the PIM system itself as much as from various experimental treatments—programming and reporting on all (instead of only some) projects and introducing annual implementation reviews and a burdensome annual evaluation review. The lesson is clear and sharp: to keep reporting short, simple and functional.

(iv) *departmentalism*. Departmental collaboration in the SRDP was improved by the system. The procedure requiring joint programming brought officers of different departments together and required them to identify and accept mutual responsibilities for action. Joint programming and the management meetings made their problems clear to one another and showed what help one department could give to another. The Area Co-ordinator emerged as a valuable ally who through his action reports and other access had means of breaking departmental bottlenecks higher up in the government machine and thereby helping his colleagues at the division level.

(v) *top-down targetry*. The essence of joint programming is that staff agree and set themselves their own targets, sitting together as colleagues. There are situations in which there may be good reasons why targets should be set higher up—for example when supplies of inputs are based on disaggregation of what is available centrally. But for most projects there is scope for staff to decide for themselves what they can achieve. Initial experience with the SRDP was that staff set themselves quite high targets and generally did not take refuge in low target-setting in order that their achievements might look better. Through drawing up

50

their own programmes and deciding for themselves what they could try to achieve, they developed a greater commitment to the projects for which they were responsible.

(vi) *inadequate resources*. Joint programming helped to identify the resources needed, and through the presence of the funding officer from headquarters, ensured that someone at the top knew what was required. The action report made the Area Co-ordinator identify and show up the reasons for failures and delays, thus giving local-level staff a direct means of telling the decision-makers at the top what problems and constraints they faced and how they could be overcome. The programming charts and action reports picked up and dramatized the damaging effects of the late fund releases which so often wreck rural development projects, particularly in agriculture with its seasonal deadlines which make timeliness so vital.

(vii) *ineffective work programming*. The joint programming exercise forced staff into thinking about their work commitments for the coming year and made it easier to recognize that there might be overloads at certain periods. The programming chart required and embodied systematic action planning for each project, showing who had to do what and when. And in practice the "how" of programming was also taken care of in the discussion generated by the procedure for the programming and management meetings.

A further benefit from the PIM system, identified by Chabala and others in their independent evaluation, was the creation of mechanisms of collegial control among divisional officers. Following their examination of the system as it was working in four areas, they wrote:

On the formal level there is very little that an officer's colleagues can do to make him co-operate with them or meet his commitments. Yet we found that with very few exceptions officers do make a real effort to meet their fellows' expectations. The existence of public records of their performance is enough to make them conform. (This is a general behaviour pattern. See Blau and Scott, 1963:178—180). No officer wishes to be criticized by his colleagues in the monthly management meeting ... The clear definition of responsibilities forms a basis on which criticism can be based with few possibilities of the officer's "passing the buck". Equally important are more informal social pressures. An officer's social standing among his peers is bound to suffer if he lets them down or is lazy or incompetent. This is particularly true in a small and isolated community, where they depend on one another both on and off the job.

(Chabala, Kiiru, Mukuna and Leonard, 1973:8)

Another benefit was an increased capability and confidence among local-level staff, who were encouraged to change from being the passive and obedient servants of their superiors to becoming thinking and responsible planners of project implementation, using their local knowledge and setting their own targets and agreeing to be judged against them. The programming exercise also had value in helping participants to understand how the government system worked and in improving their competence in operating it. Even where transfers were frequent, the immediacy of implementation following the programming exercise encouraged among staff a responsible realism which was often missing from plan formulation with its longer time horizons and "never never" touch. PIM showed itself, in fact, to be a device for staff development, quite apart from its more direct operational value.

A final benefit which deserves to be mentioned is building up the role, usefulness and credibility of an action co-ordinator. In the case of the SRDP, the Area Co-ordinators were enabled by the PIM system to legitimate themselves vis-a-vis their colleagues in other departments, and to appear to them as peers with power, through action reports and access to senior officers, to be allies who could help break departmental bottlenecks. The PIM system, indeed, was central to the Area Co-ordinators' initial effectiveness.

Like any system of management procedures, PIM has weaknesses and costs, some of which have already been mentioned. In addition it is sensitive to personality. The evaluation by Chabala and others (1973) found the system working well in three areas but badly in a fourth, which they attributed partly to this factor. Ideally the introduction of a system such as PIM should be accompanied or followed by management training to make participants aware of some of the implications of the system and of their attitudes and behaviour in operating it. Again, if many projects are programmed and reported on, the action report becomes long and less useful: it is important to use the system selectively only for those projects of higher priority, which involve several departments, or which involve several levels in a hierarchy. Some staff may complain, as did some headquarters officers responsible for SRDP fund releases, about the time required to travel to rural areas and programme jointly with field staff. The question, however, is one of weighing these and other costs against those of not having such a system. The costs of delayed fund releases in damage to staff morale, in lost credibility of government, in lagging implementation and underspending of funds voted for rural development, are so high that the question is whether a government can afford *not* to send funding officers to such meetings. More generally, the issue is whether a government can afford *not* to have a management system for programming and implementation.

5. Principles and replication

Some of the main principles incorporated in the PIM system are:

- a procedure requiring joint programming by all those responsible for implementation;
- staff taking part in setting their own work targets;
- collegial sanctions against poor work;
- lean and functional reports;
- communication direct from the implementer to the point of bottleneck or delay;
- functional meetings used sparingly;
- sophistication in simplicity.

These principles could be embodied in many different systems of procedures. Just as we borrowed from the Malaysian redbook system in order to put together PIM, so parts of PIM might be used in devising other systems for other circumstances. Nor are all the parts of the system essential to one another. The programming exercise could be held without the management meetings, although there might be a natural pressure to institute them. The whole system could be closed lower down, without communication up the hierarchy, although (unless all the resources required were available locally and at the discretion of the local-level staff) this might allow delays and bottlenecks higher in the machine to wreck local-level projects. The parts required, their details, and how they link together, should be devised afresh for each set of circumstances.

As they stand, the PIM principles and system require three conditions if they are to be put to work elsewhere. First, a deviser and tester of procedures is needed to appraise local conditions, to design appropriate procedures, to introduce them, and through continuous monitoring and evaluation in collaboration with those who are operating them, to modify them and introduce simplifications.

Second, an action co-ordinator must be identified in each area in which the management system is to be used. He should be a person who can call together staff of different departments, who can handle the programming exercise, and who has the drive and initiative to make a system of meetings and action reports work. Possible candidates can be found in most rural areas: the District Officers I, or the District Development and District Planning Officers (as and when they are appointed) in Kenya; the District Directors of Development in Tanzania; the District Development Officers in Botswana; the District Development Secretaries in Lesotho; and so on.

Third, the procedures should be introduced with a combination of authority and flexibility. The requirement that they be carried out should issue with an authority which ensures that all staff who are concerned will take part. At the same time, the possibility of modifying the procedures in the light of experience should be kept open. Adoption on a trial pilot basis, with authority from the senior ministry in government, is probably the ideal.

Finally, the approach outlined above is not a panacea. It has no monopoly of wisdom. It is open to abuses and malfunctioning. It can cease to work if it lacks a supporting drive from the centre. It can degenerate into empty ritual. But when all that has been said, our best judgment is that in the countries of Eastern Africa a system of this sort is well worth trying and should lead to a sharpening and increased effectiveness in the implementation of government development programmes in rural areas.

III. Managing Invisible Men: Procedures for Field Staff

And cast ye the unprofitable servant into outer darkness; there shall be weeping and gnashing of teeth.

Matthew xxv, 30.

1. Performance, problems, potential

Most African countries have established large field staffs and support them at great cost relative to their national incomes. They work in various departments and organizations, including animal production services, community development, crop production services, education, fisheries, forestry, game, health, lands, local government, veterinary services, and water. These departments are usually organized as territorial hierarchies, as pyramids with their apexes in the capital city, subordinate levels at province or region, district and sometimes subdistrict, and finally a broad base of field workers who are geographically dispersed with responsibilities for services in the lowest sub-areas. It is with this broad base of the pyramid, with those who are last in the line, living and working in rural "outer darkness" and almost invisible from the distant top, that we are concerned: with those government staff who are in direct contact with the rural people and through whom most government policies and programmes for rural development are mediated.

At one time it seemed right to describe these staff as "forgotten men" (Chambers 1966), for as late as the mid-1960's they had been largely ignored by those researching into the development process in Eastern Africa. But in the latter 1960's and early 1970's agricultural specialists, sociologists, political scientists and students of public administration in both East and West Africa carried out a number of useful studies which illuminated performance, problems and opportunities in agricultural extension. Studies of junior agricultural staff were conducted in Tanzania by Cliffe and others (1968), Saylor (1970) and

55

Van Velsen (1973); in Kenya by Leonard (1970a; 1970b; 1970c; *et al.* 1971; 1972a; 1972b) and Watts (1968; 1970a); in Uganda by Vail (1970) and Watts (1969, 1970b; 1970c; 1971); in Western Nigeria by Harrison (1969) and Kidd (1968; 1971); and in Eastern Nigeria by Hursch, Röling and Kerr (1968). These studies provide an excellent basis, which has not yet been fully exploited, for comparison and generalization about the bottom levels of agricultural field administration. It is unfortunate for field staffs and governments alike that the research carried out in East Africa appears, at the time of writing at least, to have had but little impact on policies. In this chapter we will draw selectively on these and a few other studies to emphasize certain findings, but this is no substitute for the serious comparative study of them which deserves to be made; nor is this a reason for neglecting the many other important findings and conclusions of these works.

The focus in this chapter will be mainly on agricultural extension, though also drawing on some experience with community development. There are several reasons for this concentration on one activity and its associated department: it has been more widely studied than any other; the numbers of staff are greater than in most other departments; and they have a major potential role in rural development and in policies designed to promote equity. Moreover, despite official pronouncements about equity and the desire to help the poorer people, it has only been through some settlement schemes in Kenya and through *ujamaa vijijini* in Tanzania that there have been to our knowledge any major development initiatives intended permanently to assist poorer people in the rural areas. The extension services have remained strongly biased towards the richer and more progressive farmers; and in East Africa, with the exception of work carried out in settlement schemes, in *ujamaa*, in the Kenya SRDP (Röling and Chege 1972; Chege and Röling 1972), and in a few credit programmes, we are not aware of any serious attempt to shift the attention of agricultural extension staff towards the less-well-off farmers. In the meantime the potential contribution to accelerated growth and equity which could be made by the large numbers of agricultural fieldworkers is perceived but dimly from the centre, and as with many dim perceptions is based on myth, prejudice and stereotype more than knowledge. Because the fieldworkers in their rural outer darkness are almost invisible to those at the top, their potential is, in our experience, grossly underestimated. It is the main purpose of this chapter to suggest some first steps of an approach to releasing and canalizing that potential the better to promote development and equity in rural areas.

There is a widespread belief that field staff are idle, venal, and incompetent. Guy Hunter has well written of Africa and Asia together about the

quality of poorly educated and badly paid staff at the lowest level of all. It is these small men who come into direct contact with the village and the farmer. They cannot be given discretions, are usually badly supervised, often operate with written instructions which are out of relation with what it is possible or sensible to do in their local circumstance. They are often seen as emissaries of "government" enforcing mysterious and even senseless regulations, who must be bribed or evaded in order that the ordinary needs of village life can be met—at best a particularly tiresome form of local taxation, at worst a petty tyranny.

(1969; 202)

This description applies more to Asia than to Africa, and more to those staff concerned with tax collection and regulatory duties than those involved in positive development. It is, all the same, in general harmony with the widespread conviction in Ministries of Agriculture that the lowest levels of agricultural extension staff are virtually useless, "dead wood", incapable of giving the sophisticated advice which is the only advice worth giving, and devoted not to the development of their areas but to their own farms and interests. The prescription which then follows is that many of them should be compulsorily retired and a fresh start made with younger, better educated, and, it is assumed, more effective staff.

There is much evidence to justify these views. Many studies have pointed to what Moris (1972:135) calls "the relaxed pace of field administration at the bottom levels". Studies in Tanzania (Cliffe et al. 1968:3) and Western Nigeria (Harrison 1969:200) have both found extension workers only spending about five hours a day working (including travel). The number of visits to individual farms was found to be 10 per week in Tanzania (Cliffe et al. 1968:6) and 20 per month in one part of Kenya with only an average of 1.75 farmers visited on those days wholly devoted to individual farm visits (Leonard 1972b: 19). In Western Nigeria Harrison reported "widespread minor misconduct such as absence from duty and the covert refusal to live in one's extension zone" (1969:280). Mbithi quotes an agricultural officer having to chase his junior staff from market places, "pombe (beer) parties", and aimless cycling all over the countryside (1973:111).

57

Extension work has been found, not surprisingly, to be biased toward places close to where the extension worker lives: Kidd noted in Western Nigeria that staff concentrated their efforts on a few relatively accessible villages (1968:4); Vail observed in an experimental programme in Uganda a hyperconcentration on one section of the project area (1970: [i]); and our own work in Mbere Division in Kenya showed a similar pattern. Staff meetings have been found to be concerned heavily with personal and financial matters (Cliffe et al. 1968:17; Kidd 1971:86—7; Saylor 1970:10). Leonard even found that the more meetings were held, the poorer the work effort became as a result of counter-organization and work restriction by the staff (1972b:20). Moreover, reports submitted by staff are often of little use for decision-making at higher levels (Cliffe et al. 1968:18). In the view of one Tanzanian researcher, extension workers "work fairly short hours, miss work days, spend much time on travel, wage payments, reports and other activities not directly productive" (Cliffe et al. 1968:14).

A further criticism, levelled mainly by academic observers, is that extension workers are allied with and devote their attention largely to the better-off farmers. The Tanzanian extension agent who was reported to have "spent the day weeding the Area Commissioner's cotton shamba" (Cliffe et al. 1968:14) may have been exceptional, but there is overwhelming evidence from all over the world that extension benefits go mainly to those who are already more prosperous. Van Velsen (1973) has argued that social and economic reciprocities between the staff—"wasitafu"— and the local elite are a major factor in this bias, while Leonard (1972a:14), drawing on evidence from Western Kenya, considers that a combination of factors are responsible, including extension ideology stressing the progressive farmer approach, the psychological attractiveness of visiting farmers who are receptive, a weak commitment to work, the pattern of farmer demand for services, and a distorted perception by extension workers of the rural situation which leads them to believe that progressive farmers are a higher proportion of all farmers than is the case. There is general agreement among these observers that extension workers often get too close to the client system (Mbithi 1973:111) and that the bias towards the progressives is undesirable. Although the academics and the government agriculturalists may disagree on this point of policy, there is a consensus that extension staff do much less work than they could, and this supports the common central government view that they are lazy and unprofitable servants, deserving to be disciplined, sacked, or compelled to work harder.

The view seen by the servants themselves from their rural outer darkness is, however, very different. There are striking similarities in the findings of the many studies which have been carried out. The problems and disincentives facing field, and particularly agricultural, staff can be considered under three headings: terms of service and living conditions; working conditions; and supervision.

In the first place, agricultural extension staff widely perceive their terms of service to be poor. They are usually secure in their posts, but their pay and allowances are less than those of their peers working for parastatal or private sector organizations in similar fields (such as tobacco extension in Nigeria or tea extension in Kenya). Their allowances are often delayed in payment. Housing is often not provided or is not of a quality which accords with their aspirations. Promotion prospects are poor and are widely believed to be related to family or tribal connections rather than to work performance. Good work is not seen to be rewarded and a low work output is not seen to be penalized. In short, there is little economic or career incentive for hard or good work.

Second, working conditions are physically hard and often personally frustrating. The climate is usually either hot or wet or both. Where there is heavy rain, raincoats are not provided. Lack of transport is a recurrent problem which rarely receives a sympathetic hearing. Effectively to cover the geographical areas of responsibility is often impossible without a motorcycle, but in practice staff usually have to travel by bicycle or on foot and spend much of their time doing so. Extension programmes are often badly designed or inappropriate, and extension workers find themselves advising farmers to adopt practices which are ecologically unsuitable, which they themselves would not adopt, and which would not be economic for any farmer rash enough to try them out (Joy 1969:3; Otieno and Belshaw 1964; Okai, n.d.; Heyer, Ireri and Moris 1971:58—59). The logistical back-up with inputs such as seeds and fertilizers is essential but difficult to organize and often does not occur in time (Vail 1970). There may be either a lack of instructions from the centre, or an overload of programmes flowing out from the centre without any systematic appraisal of compatibility in their demands on staff time, the later ones burying the earlier. We observed one case where a young farmers' programme was suddenly introduced, diverting extension staff off their planned work. Many young farmers' clubs were formed and land was cleared; but the seeds required were never delivered, leaving the staff, the young farmers and the population in general demoralized and confirmed in their cynicism about centrally-derived government programmes.

Third, supervision is often erratic, almost non-existent, or poor. Staff may be subject to rare and unpredictable visits in which quick decisions are made and judgements arrived at on the basis of inadequate appraisal; or they may be scarcely visited at all, like the Bwana Shamba (agricultural extension worker) in Tanzania who claimed that no superior officer had been to see him in the field for four years (Cliffe *et al.* 1968:18). In most, perhaps all, countries transport for supervisors is inadequate: it would be difficult, perhaps impossible, to find a country where at some stage sensible proposals for providing superiors with motorcycles has not been turned down by the Treasury or Ministry of Finance. When the supervisor does visit the field-workers, he may engage in purely social interaction: no less than 83 per cent of Saylor's Bwana Shamba respondents agreed with the statement "When my senior officer visits me in the field it is usually a social visit and unrelated to my work" (1970:15). A monthly meeting is usually held, but it competes for time and attention with pay and its aftermath and in any case much of the business discussed relates to allowances, housing, and other personal matters and not to the work of agricultural extension. In spite of this tendency at monthly meetings, extension staff feel that their grievances and needs are for the most part not met and indeed not even communicated to the higher levels at which decisions could be taken about them.

This picture may appear overdrawn. It must be qualified in certain respects: much of it is based on research carried out some years ago; much of the evidence comes from Tanzania in the late 1960's, which for various reasons, including the wide geographical dispersal of staff, may have had lower performance than usual; the researchers who are being quoted provided staff with opportunities to complain, with a shoulder to weep on, and may sometimes have identified with their informants; and this selective summary has picked on negative rather than positive aspects. All the same, even discounting for these biases, this evidence does show the extension worker in a different light from the usual central government view. A comparison with peasant farmers may help at this stage. Peasant farming behaviour once called conservative has been so thoroughly understood and so thoroughly interpreted as rational that peasants now appear almost as embodiments of the eighteenth-century enlightenment; and it has become anathema in social science circles to suggest that peasants as a group can be categorised as "lazy". Junior government field workers are somewhat similar. As with any group of people, some are industrious and some are not. What does emerge, however, is that much of the inactivity and the low work output can be understood as a rational response to a combination of terms of service, living conditions, working conditions, and supervision. Neither penalties nor rewards provide strong incentives for better performance. In these circumstances, the potential and abilities of staff lie largely dormant, a latent but unrealized resource. Staff could work eight or more hours a day instead of five. They could visit more than just the progressive elite of farmers. They could cover villages and farmers more distant from the places where they live. That they do not do these things is largely because they are rational. The question is how to change their work environment so that it becomes equally rational for them to work harder and better.

Many diagnoses and prescriptions have been put forward. Hunter (1970a) has made many recommendations which defy a brief summary. Harrison (1969:280—1) has carefully argued for Western Nigeria that positive rewards in the form of increments and promotions based on performance are likely to be the most effective incentives for field agricultural staff. This point of view finds support from Leonard's observation (1972b:19—20) that salary differentials between staff levels (a hangover from the colonial European-African distinction) coupled with poor promotion opportunities are powerful irritants and disincentives for staff. Many smaller reforms regarding transport, allowances, housing and clothing could also help. But recommendations on points such as these have been made repeatedly and usually in vain. They are important; but they are difficult to get action on, involving as they do protracted negotiations with a Ministry of Finance whose officers have even less sympathy for these unprofitable servants in outer darkness than have the senior officers in Ministries of Agriculture. In the meantime, while such negotiations are going on, it is worth asking whether motivation and performance can be improved in other ways.

A final point of great importance is how good the extension advice being offered is for the farmer. This crucial precondition for extension success is far too easily and far too often overlooked. First class training of staff, consummate mastery of the most recent fashions in methods of communication, sensible terms of service, reasonable working conditions, good supervision, strong personal motivation—

all these are useless, indeed precisely worse than useless, unless the advice given benefits the farmer. Conversely if there is a really good innovation to promote, the chances are good that staff morale and performance will be high. A prior condition to gaining benefits from the approach described below is that research shall be organized to produce innovations which make sense to the farmers. Without good content in extension programmes, every other measure of reform is in vain.

2. The primary thrust: Supervision and work planning

Most observers identify poor supervision as a major factor in poor motivation and low work performance. Hursh, Röling and Kerr, having studied agricultural extension organization in 71 villages in Eastern Nigeria, concluded that:

Agricultural extension agents often live in villages under conditions that foster lethargy, with no meaningful communication with superiors, inadequate supervision and advice. All these factors create feelings of personal alienation and dislocation. Strategies to expand the efficiency and vitality of the extension service would have to include improvements in the interaction between change agency bureaucracy and extension agent in the village.

(1968:159)

In Tanzania, Saylor noted that officers themselves felt they were poorly supervised (1970:10) and Cliffe and others (1968:17) concluded that for the most part field workers were left to decide for themselves which crop to emphasize, what operations and improvements to stress, which farmers to concentrate on, and how to organize their time. The common lack of supervision in the general extension service is contrasted with the tighter systems in one-crop organizations such as the Nigerian Tobacco Company (Harrison 1969: 213, 233), the Kenya Tea Development Authority (Heyer, Ireri, and Moris 1971:59; Moris 1972: 130—133), and the paddy-growing Mwea Irrigation Settlement in Kenya (Chambers and Moris 1973), with their combinations of clearly defined tasks, strict discipline, cross-checks on performance, and close supervision of field workers. There are many variables involved here including the higher salaries, lower job security, and more easily routinized tasks of these organizations. There must also be reservations about the effectiveness of the supervisory systems (Leonard 1972b: 22). Nevertheless, observers agree that staff in these organizations do work harder and more effectively than in the general extension service, and that supervision is one important contributing factor.

Two linked problems are staff evaluation and work planning. The perception by field staff that their prospects for promotion and other benefits depend mainly on personal and ethnic factors rather than on work performance, and the crucial importance they attach to salaries and allowances, combine to make it a sound strategy for them to try to please those in authority over them and to try to secure benefits through ethnic networks rather than through performing well on the job. (This is, of course, even more pronounced when there is little substantive work to do.) At the same time, their work programmes are often unplanned. Oyugi quotes a district head of department in Kenya as saying of his locational staff "They do not know where they are going until they have reached there. And they do not know what they are going to do until they have actually begun to do it" (1973:14—15). This may be a little extreme and a little unfair; but the malaise of unplanned work is widespread.

In itself, closer supervision will not necessarily overcome these problems. It has to be linked with closer specification of the work to be done and then with fair evaluation of the performance of that work. A prior condition for the effective operation of any system of incentives is an "objective and rigorous method of monitoring junior staff performance" (Leonard 1972b:31). Such a method can most easily be developed through the careful planning of work. As Kidd says for Western Nigeria:

Each staff member needs a clear definition of (1) what he should do, (2) how this relates to what other staff do for clientele, and (3) to what goals he should be aiming. Perhaps the best way to achieve this is to have supervisory staff work individually with subordinates and help them set realistic goals and outline the work required to achieve those goals ... (1968:14)

Similarly, Joy points out the need of extension staff for "fully worked out routines" (1969:7). Such work planning carries its own direct benefits in increased efficiency; but it is also a precondition for a system of evaluating individual performance by results, since it specifies what results the individual is expected to achieve. But observers almost invariably stop short of stating just how these changes should be achieved—how staff should be supervised, goals set, work planned, routines worked out, and staff evaluated.

These problems are related to the system of communication within the organization. At its worst this takes two forms. The first is a downwards flow of instructions and targets which are largely unrelated to the resources, particularly staff time, available at the grass roots. It is common to find that staff time is not thought of as a scarce or finite resource and whether it is under- or over-utilized is a matter of chance. Staff may have almost nothing to do; or they may be bombarded, like some community development workers in Kenya, by the demands of entrepreneurial departments and agencies at the centre which compete for their time and energies.

The second flow of communication is routine, ritual, unusuable, un-used and unread reports passed upwards. In Tanzania a study found that monthly reports followed a set format, that scarcely a word was changed from month to month, and that reports had little utility as a means of supervision and control (Cliffe *et al.* 1968). Reporting pathology is a topic in its own right (see for example Kulp 1970:330—1). Suffice it here to say that current reporting systems in agriculture usually incorporate routine information of doubtful reliability and rarely include sufficiently detailed statements of staff activities to enable any evaluation of performance to be made. The two information flows—instructions downwards, and routine information largely unrelated to those instructions upward—present an ironical situation in which both sides punch the air without connecting, and the most important information—the achievements and problems of field implementation—is barely touched on, if at all, in the upward flow.

Supervision, work planning, reporting and staff evaluation are all procedurally related. Any attempt to grapple realistically with the detail of procedures to handle one of these is likely, if it is to be effective, to lead into the others. This certainly was the experience in an experimental situation in the Kenya SRDP which, as the following description shows, led far from the original starting point.

3. Procedures for managing field staff

The Experimental Experience

The procedures which are described below were developed over a period of about 18 months in collaboration with the agricultural extension staff of Mbere Division in Embu District in Kenya. The experimental rationale of the SRDP provided an opportunity to devise, test and modify procedures. Since the resulting systems, or the principles on which they are based, might be considered for use elsewhere, we will first describe the situation into which they were introduced,[1] and then the sequence of experience in developing them. This may help the reader to appraise the replicability of the principles and details and also help any others who undertake similar work to make fewer mistakes and follow a shorter route than we did.

Mbere Division became the site for this work because it was an SRDP area and because it was reasonably accessible, being only some 120 kilometres to northeast of Nairobi (and some 70 kilometres southeast of Mount Kenya). It is a marginal area for agriculture, lying mostly within an altitude range between 4,000 and 2,000 feet above sea level with corresponding mean rainfalls varying from over 50 inches to under 35 inches per annum. The SRDP area was relatively sparsely populated, with 64,500 people living in 1,630 square kilometres. The principal staff with whom the procedures were developed were two Assistant Agricultural Officers (AAOs, each with a three-year diploma in agriculture, one of whom was in charge of the division, and one of whom specialized in cotton), 3 Location Agricultural Assistants (LAAs, each with a two-year certificate in agriculture, and each in charge of one of three locations) and about 25 other agricultural staff, mainly Junior Agricultural Assistants (JAAs, with varying but lesser amounts of training) who were divided between the three locations and supervised by the LAAs. The main crops which were the concern of the extension workers in the upper higher-rainfall areas were cotton, tobacco, Mexico 142 peabeans and Katumani maize; and in the lower areas cotton, Katumani maize, and castor. In parallel with the agricultural extension staff was a less numerous livestock staff consisting of an Animal Husbandry Assistant (AHA) in charge with about 12 Junior Animal Husbandry Assistants (JAHAs) under him. The live-

---

1. See also pages 20—21.

stock staff were concerned mainly with periodical campaigns for inoculation, castration and censuses and with routine attendance at cattle dips.[1]

We began at the District level with an interest in agricultural data, information flows, and planning. There we found a set of practices which was fairly typical for Kenya. District targets for crop acreages were either set at the district level or received from the provincial level. They were then progressively disaggregated by the District Agricultural Officer, the AAO and the LAAs down to the level of the JAAs, each of whom was given a target acreage to achieve. Targets tended to escalate year by year without any very close relation to what had been achieved in previous years. Feedback on actual achievement was largely through a reporting system in which each month each JAA submitted a report to his LAA, who then compiled a report for his AAO, who then compiled a further report for the District Agricultural Officer. The reporting formats at the lower levels were far from uniform. Scepticism about the validity of the acreage figures so reported was widespread but they did nevertheless give some idea of orders of magnitude.

In an attempt to assess the feasibility of the targets set and with the assistance of the District Agricultural Officer, we calculated the monthly workloads which the targets implied for extension staff in one location. The outcome was startling, varying from 18 per cent to 474 per cent of the staff time that was available (Belshaw and Chambers 1971, appendix D). In the setting of targets staff time was obviously not taken into account as a scarce resource, the use of which would force choices between alternatives. Indeed, the practice throughout the Ministry of Agriculture was that a series of priority programmes flowed out from the centre, one after another, quite independent even of these district targets, each subsequent programme tending to bury its predecessors. The effects of these various unrealistic demands on junior field staff can be imagined. We ourselves observed that the young farmers' programme which was suddenly and unexpectedly introduced from Nairobi took up two-thirds of the time of a JAA at the cost of the other work that he was to have done. In the face of such unpredictable and incompatible demands, it was scarcely surprising that the junior field staff should tend towards a passive fatalism. What

1. For further description and discussion of the staff of Mbere Division, see Brokensha and Nellis 1971.

was remarkable, indeed, in these difficult circumstances, was that they worked as hard and well, as they did.

As we found it, the main defects of the system appeared to be:

- top-down targetry which was usually unrealistic
- no systematic choices of priority between competing demands on staff time
- no organized work planning for field staff
- little feedback on staff activities to supervisors
- a lack of standard reporting procedures

An early finding was that a solution to these difficulties could not be found through better planning at the district or even the division level. The exercise of working out a year's monthly workloads for only one location took us the equivalent of between two and three laborious mandays. It was unthinkable that this should be repeated for a whole district. It seemed obvious that work planning would have to take place in the location itself. At the same time, certain types of targets had to be planned from the centre, namely, those which required inputs which were centrally supplied, examples being demonstration plots for which seed and fertilizer were needed and for which only a limited supply was available. Moreover, the Ministry of Agriculture and the District Agricultural Officer must obviously be able to exercise control over the activities of their staff. A mixed system was needed, in which certain priorities were handed down, but in which detailed work planning was based realistically on the staff time available.

We were driven to the location and the locational monthly meeting of staff as the level and occasion for innovation. Even here our path was far from straight. Initially, still concerned particularly with agricultural data, a system was introduced for reporting farm visits, with the intention of building up locational records of farms and extension contact. Each JAA made out in triplicate brief records of each visit, and was debriefed on these at the end of the month. This proved a strain on staff literacy, quickly generated a lot of paper, and was not followed through into the compiling of a location register of farms as intended. (A simpler, more ingenious and probably more workable system of recording extension contact has been suggested by Röling and Chege 1972). The lesson which we learnt, the hard way, and which it seems necessary to learn over and over again, was to keep paperwork short and simple.

Other elements in the initial system were, however, more useful. Extension workers were given small red books which they left with the farmers they visited and in which they then later recorded their subsequent visits, providing an independent check on their activities. Each extension worker also kept a small black book in which he recorded a list of farmers with whom he had contact, arranged by village, and wrote in the dates of his contacts, thus providing an easily inspected check on the extent to which he was concentrating on a small number of farmers or spreading his attentions more widely.

The red and black books, however, did not provide a means for work planning. They recorded what had been done, not what was to be done; and they were liable to bias activities towards individual farm visits to the detriment of demonstrations and other extension techniques. We therefore devised forms which could be used at the monthly location-level meetings for setting work targets for the month, and later for recording actual activities during the month. For research purposes we included spaces for the number of hours spent on different activities, including travel, but these were later dropped in the course of simplification. As we proceeded, modifying the forms month by month to a degree which we would never have anticipated, it gradually became clear that it was important both for the realism of work planning and target setting and also for motivation that staff should freely take part in the meeting and should make suggestions about the priorities and targets of their work. Towards the end of the experimental experience, under the influence of the location-level situation and also of the precepts of MBO, the procedures required that junior staff each month agree their programmes and targets freely with their supervisors.

Throughout the 18 months we were drawn again and again in the direction of requesting or requiring additional data collection. We varied the demands experimentally between the three locations. Only gradually were we prepared to recognize that much, indeed most, of the additional data would never be used unless there was a direct functional application in the location level meeting. The abandonment of the triplicate farm visit book was followed by the elimination of the recording of numbers of hours spent on different activities, and finally by an aggregate report of staff activities which was to be sent up to the district level. For although the latter looked as though it ought to be very useful for purpose of surveillance and future planning, it seemed unlikely that in practice it would make sufficient difference to decisions to justify the effort its compilation required.

We made several attempts to use the system developed for crops staff for the livestock staff, and each attempt failed. We came to realise that the livestock staff were less literate and that the work was more routine, more planned in advance, and less liable to change. A separate and simpler system was therefore devised for them, using some of the same principles. The major difference was that for crops staff work planning was by targets, whereas for the livestock staff, work planning was by days.

The descriptions which follow record the procedures which were operating early in 1973. They show that although we set out with a concern for agricultural information flows and planning we ended with a system for field staff management.

Work Planning by Targets: The Crops Staff System

A full description of the system presented as instructions to the supervisor, together with copies of forms, is given in the Appendices, p. 176 —198. The full system had five main components. These were:

(i) *a Daily Activities Record* (see Appendix, p. 193) kept by each staff member. It shows the days of the month, the numbers of days available for extension work, the extension activities planned for the period together with targets, the work carried out each day recorded on a daily basis, and a summary of achievement by the end of the period. It provides each staff member with a work plan and targets for the month but does not lay down what should be done each day, allowing for responsible and flexible allocation of time between activities by the staff member himself.

(ii) *a Location Planning Sheet* (see Appendix, p. 193) worked out by the supervisor with help from the extension staff. This shows the number of days available for extension work for each staff member in the location after deduction of days for holidays, weekends, courses and so forth. It provides for the listing of activities to be carried out and assignment of priorities between them. It is used by the supervisor in discussion with staff to determine realistic work targets.

(iii) *a Small Register* (the black book) maintained by each extension worker listing by village or other spatial grouping those farmers whom he visits and the date of each visit. The dates of successive visits are written across the page so that the frequency of visits to any one farmer can easily be seen.

(iv) *a Daily Diary* kept up by each staff member showing whom he has visited and what he has done on each day.

(v) *a Farm Visit Book* (the red book), a small cheap notebook given to each farmer who is visited and entered up by staff members whenever they visit that farmer, showing the date of the visit, what advice they have given and the signature of the visitor. In additional a Crop Data Sheet for recording the crop acreages per extension worker and the number of farmers growing the crops can be used to help in the planning of time allocations.

The system centred on a regular meeting, held monthly in the case of the trial system, at which supervision and work planning took place. Before the meeting the supervisor (the AAO in the trial system) obtained any information he might need for the next month's work planning. The meeting was held at the location level and was divided into three phases:

(i) *debriefing and supervision:* The supervisor sat down with each staff member in turn. He examined each staff member's Daily Activities Record, which showed in summary what had been done each day, his diary, which described what was done in more detail, including the names of farmers visited and what they were advised on, and his register, which had an entry against each farmer's name for each visit. They discussed in detail the work which had been done, and the extension worker was encouraged to explain problems he had encountered. The records were cross-checked between Daily Activities Record, diary and register. Any inconsistencies or errors were examined. The targets which were jointly set the month before and the achievements reported were compared and discussed. The register indicated any tendency to pay too many visits to some villages or farmers or too few to others, making it possible for the supervisor to monitor the spread of extension work and to correct imbalances.

(ii) *discussion:* When the individual debriefings and supervision were complete, any general matters were discussed.

(iii) *Joint planning:* With the help of staff members the supervisor then completed the Location Planning Sheet to show how many days each of them had available for work before the next monthly meeting. The supervisor listed the crops, crop operations and extension methods for the coming period and placed these in order of priority on the sheet, entering those targets which had already been set from above. In discussion with the staff, these pre-set targets were allocated and the days their achievement would require were deducted from each individual's total of days available as appropriate. Targets for priority operations were then discussed freely and allocated. As these were agreed, the supervisor kept a running total of days remaining for each staff member. Discretion was given to staff to take part in setting their own targets and to suggest what their work priorities should be. One way of doing this was to ask them to decide how many farm visits out of a target total should be devoted to the different crops grown in their areas. The operation continued until all the days available had been allocated. Staff members then copied down the details on their new Daily Activities Records which they took away as records of the work targets they had agreed to for the next month. They then entered what they actually did day to day until the next monthly meeting.

In between meetings the supervisor at location level was meant to visit staff, check that they were keeping their records accurately and up-to-date, inspect some of the farm visit books held by individual farmers and cross-check these against the records maintained by the staff.

Work Planning by Days: Systems for Livestock and Community Development Staff

A full description of the system presented as instructions to a supervisor of livestock staff together with a copy of the form used is given in Appendix H, p. 194.

The procedures for livestock staff were similar to those for crops staff but simpler and less flexible. Compared with crops staff the work of livestock staff was less liable to unexpected alteration, more routine (for example with attendance at dips on certain days of the week), and more centrally planned in advance for campaigns for inoculations, castrations, and inseminations and for stock censuses. The numbers of staff were also smaller, so that the supervisor could spend more time planning on an individual basis. In these conditions, work planning was best carried out by determining activities day by day.

The monthly meeting followed a similar sequence, starting with individual debriefing using the Daily Work Plan and Report Form from the previous month. This showed what was planned, what actually happened, and the various figures and data on which reports were required. Entries were checked against the staff member's diary and details discussed. After a period for the discussion of any general matters, the next month was planned. The days until the next meeting were entered on the form and then entries made for leave, courses and pay; centrally planned campaigns; routine activities; and meetings and demonstrations, in that order. Through discussion between the staff member and the supervisor, the days remaining were then divided up between other activities. The staff member left the meeting with the Work Plan showing what he was to do on each day for the next month and then filled it in daily with what he actually did.

A system of planning by days was also proposed for community development staff but for somewhat different reasons. Livestock staff had regular routines and campaigns which took up much of their time so that an 'advance engagements' type of work programme was sensible. Community development staff, in contrast, usually lacked regular routines on fixed days. Those working in two SRDP areas, (Tetu and Mbere), however, were under heavy pressure from competing demands made on their time. From the centre they were harried by high-powered visits from energetic entrepreneurial specialists all seeking to promote their particular programmes, whether functional literacy, family planning, local participation in planning, locational leaders' seminars, better family living, or whatever. In the field their time was demanded by Chiefs and headmen to assist with self-help groups, by women's groups, and by various grass-roots organizations. Moreover the programming carried out through the PIM system had given each SRDP area targets for completion by deadlines which they were engaged in trying to achieve. Any programmes arranged with local groups were liable to be disrupted by a sudden descent from Nairobi of some specialist enthusiast, and heavy transport costs were entailed in sending vehicles to cancel meetings, incidentally damaging the credibility of community development in the process. Faced with this competition for their time, community development workers needed a procedure for self-defence, a means of rationing the demands made on their time and of ordering priorities between them.

In these circumstances there was more reason than ever for treating those who were last in the hierarchy as first: for regarding the time of junior staff as the scarce resource, requiring "bottom-up" programming. The system proposed was that each CDA should come to the locational monthly meeting having listed dates of meetings and commitments provisionally arranged at the local level; and that central entrepreneurs (from Nairobi, from Province, from District) should by the time of the meeting have informed the supervisor (the ACDO) of any dates when they intended to visit or had planned campaigns in the area. At the meeting these dates and commitments would be reconciled and programmes, including some spare days, would be drawn up for all staff on a day by day basis for the month, stencilled, and immediately despatched to all levels concerned. Subsequent to the meeting, any senior officer or entrepreneur wishing to visit the area would be requested to fit in with the existing planned programme. The ACDO was required to list in his monthly report all programme disruptions, stating why they had occurred and who had caused them. The proposed system also simplified reporting, using a standard form in a supervisory debriefing at the monthly meeting.

4. Benefits, costs and caveats

These procedural systems centre on supervision and work planning. They were designed for particular needs and conditions and contain elements which are particularistic. Other systems might have been worked out for the same conditions and might have been more effective, but these were the best we could devise. Throughout the discussion which follows the reader is asked to bear in mind that they represent an example of learning on the job for the researchers, albeit with continual feedback from the staff operating the systems; and that the underlying principles (see page 78) may be more important than the details. Nevertheless it is by examining the details that the possible benefits and costs can best be evaluated and useful principles teased out.

At the operating level the main elements in this work planning approach to field staff management are:

- a regular management meeting held between supervisor and field workers
- a procedure for the joint preparation by supervisor and field worker of a work plan based on the days available for work during the period between meetings
- supervision and communication through discussion at the meeting of a record of work done or a report or both
- standardized reporting to streamline report preparation and handling.

The most obvious possible benefits of such systems are interrelated:
- improved *operational control* of staff, making it easier to get them

to do what they should do
- improved field staff *performance* through supervision, participation in work planning, and harder work
- improved *knowledge of what staff do* with a feedback to personnel policies, programme design, staffing practices, etc.
- improved *planning through data collection and communication* with a feedback to policy

Whether or to what extent these benefits accrue is highly sensitive to the style of management and supervision. The systems are radical in giving priority to the time and energy of the fieldworker and enabling him to take part in planning his work and targets. The procedures are designed to make this happen. But there is evidence from other organizations which indicate dangers in this approach. Blau and Scott have pointed out that "Emphasis in an organization on conformity with operating procedures discourages the exercise of initiative and the willingness to assume responsibility" (1963:129). Moreover, they found (ibid: 151) that authoritarian supervisors are the most procedure-oriented ones. In the context of African field administration, Moris (1972:135—6) has argued convincingly that top-down pressures for higher achievement can be dysfunctional. With these work planning procedures, there are obvious dangers: that supervisors will not encourage participation and will use the meetings to issue orders; that staff activities will be biased towards those which are quantifiable, reportable, and targeted and away from other more qualitative and possibly more important activities; that work performance and other information will be distorted or falsified to give a misleading impression of achievement; that the form of activities will be substituted for the substance—for example by extension workers going to a farm to sign the book and not to give the farmer advice; that the procedures will degenerate into ritual, performed because they have been performed before but without evaluation of their use; that staff will cease to exercise discretion and initiative, but rather concentrate on the letter of their instructions; that they will not vary their work to fit local conditions.

This list is formidable and daunting. But a crucial point is that the procedures are designed to encourage participation and to routinize it. They are also designed to make sure that targets and plans are realistic. The principle of MBO—that staff should set their work targets jointly with their supervisors—is required by the rules for operating the procedures. The procedures themselves are participatory. But whether this is effective depends heavily on the supervisor's personal style. If he is domineering, dogmatic and authoritarian, the system can be expected to run off course and either crash or grind along slowly in the wrong direction. If, on the other hand, he is firm, but humane, democratic and open in his style, then the anticipated benefits have a chance to be realized. An obvious implication is that ideally management training should become part of any large-scale programme of lower-level reforms in management procedures.

These dangers relate to staff evaluation. One part of MBO is evaluation by results. These procedural systems, if they operate well, should provide monthly information on "results"—work carried out, targets achieved, and so forth. But several caveats are needed here. Often, particularly in agriculture, the "results" are partly or largely beyond the control of the extension worker. Whether farmers adopt a new practice may be unrelated to his excellence or industry. One extension worker may have receptive farmers; another may be up against a brick wall. Again, the "results" are largely self-reported and difficult to verify. In the crops system, to be sure, there are cross-checks and the impression is strong that serious falsification did not take place as staff almost invariably reported a mixture of over- and under-achievements of targets. But any recognized and regular evaluation of staff in terms of performance which they report themselves, and which is not verifiable and verified, is likely to discriminate in favour of liars and against honest men. In contrast with the industrial situations for which MBO has been developed, field situations are characterized by staff who are dispersed, difficult to supervise and whose achievements are difficult to check. One conclusion is that following what may be called the Leonard Principle,[1] preference should be given to those tasks which are easily verifiable, such as result demonstrations in agriculture. Another conclusion is that verification and cross checks should themselves be required procedures. But even so, with dispersed field staff, evaluation by results is bound to remain difficult.

A further implication is that very great care should be taken by the supervisor over the manner in which he debriefs his staff on their previous month's work. On the one hand, if he reprimands and disciplines where reported performance is low he will mutilate the system and it will cease to work for him; on the other hand, if he is completely

[1] Put forward by David K. Leonard.

permissive, staff will realize that it does not make any difference what they do. He has to balance on a tightrope. In practice, the supervisors concerned in the experimental situation steered a middle course of mild reprimand, moderate praise, and restrained exhortation. The outcome was that reporting appeared to be honest but that staff did feel a definite pressure on them to work. In addition, while there was no formal evaluation by results, the monthly meetings, in particular the debriefing, did give the supervisor a strong impression of the activities and competence of their staff members.

If the style of the meeting and of supervision is firm but humane, democratic and open, and if the procedural system has been well designed, then four benefits can reasonably be expected: improved performance; improved operational control; improved knowledge of what staff do; and improved planning through data collection and communication.

First, there should be an improvement in staff performance. Any sense of isolation, of supervisors not caring whether work is done or not, should be reduced. Supervisors should be forced by the system into seeing that there is a meaningful set of programmes of work. Low morale from impossible overloads on the one hand or from low demands on the other should be avoided. Motivation to work should be improved in several ways, including a sense of responsibility in setting work targets and arranging work plans, the knowledge that work is being monitored, and the requirement to report on and justify what has been done during the month. Field workers should also feel that the debriefing system gives them an opportunity to explain to their supervisor in some detail the difficulties which they face in the field. There may also be an increased sense that good work will be known about higher in the hierarchy with the hope that this may influence promotion prospects. In sum, fieldworkers should be better motivated and should work harder.

Second, operational control of staff should be improved. New priority programmes can be fed straight into the monthly planning of work. At the end of the month there should then be a feedback on what has actually happened, making adjustments possible. The chances of actions in the field diverging from intentions higher up should be reduced. Field operations should be more predictably manipulable, a fact of importance in introducing new programmes which may be inherently difficult for staff to carry out, such as attempts to reach the smaller less-well-off farmers.

Third, a related benefit should be improved knowledge of what staff actually do. There is a dilemma here over how far up the hierarchy staff activities should be reported. With the crops system, the information closed at the level of the supervisor, whose knowledge was certainly better than before. But if the information is to go higher, there must be a mechanism for making use of it to justify the costs of preparation and transmission. This knowledge has potential importance as a means of dispelling the widespread prejudice in the centre that field staff do very little and of securing attention and remedies for their problems. There is also a potential benefit in future programme planning, through a greater knowledge of the implementation capacity which is available at field level, though one may be sceptical about the chances of such information being used. Finally, field staff can be protected through these procedures from unjust criticism: the farm visit book can be used to show that they actually did visit; the diary can show what other activities were undertaken; the community development monthly plan of work and report can show how much low output is due to unprogrammed interruptions; and so forth. The systems can, thus, not only show what staff do; they can also give them a weapon for self-defence.

Fourth, planning should be improved through streamlined data collection and its communication. Where more than one report is compiled, they can be combined. Where statistical data is required, a standard form, easy to fill in and easy to collate from, can be used. Unnecessary data collection can be eliminated. These are glib injunctions. But they can be implemented independently of other changes and are relatively easy reforms to carry out. In addition, data can be compiled which will be useful for future work and economic planning. For example, the registers compiled and kept up-to-date in the crops system provided a list of farmers contacted which could be used in deciding future extension approaches.

But of course, even if they are operated correctly, these systems have costs. They take up staff time. The crops meeting, once mastered by staff, took between two and five hours, effectively absorbing a day. There are also costs in paper, notebooks, and postage, though perhaps these are trivial. There are costs in the foregone uses of staff time absorbed in keeping records. There are latent costs in the many pitfalls into which procedural systems like these can slide. Nevertheless, the key question may be, as with the PIM system, not so much whether the system can be afforded, but rather whether a government can afford *not* to have systems on lines such as these. What does seem unquestionable is that much more experimental work is needed in order to build up experience and a repertoire of techniques on which to draw.

5. Principles, applications and rural equity

In considering applications of approaches such as these to field staff management, it is useful to stand back and to try and see what principles lie behind the detail. In summary, the argument and its conclusions are as follows. Field staff are dispersed and almost invisible. Supervision is difficult. A high degree of motivation, responsibility and initiative are needed if they are to work well. But field workers are presumed to be low calibre and lazy. This view is, however, self-validating. It is partly because they are treated as low calibre and lazy that their performance is poor. By treating them as responsible, by giving them a part in defining work plans for themselves, by giving them satisfying tasks, and by a system of supervision which brings their performance to the notice of their supervisors, their behaviour will change for the better. Although complementary reforms in terms of service, promotion prospects, and other personnel matters are desirable, an early improvement can be achieved through the introduction of systems of management procedures designed and tested for specific situations. For field workers the basic assumptions or principles are:

1. field staff are responsible workers who will respond to management and supervision which gives them a part in drawing up their own work plans and setting their own work targets.

2. work planning is desirable as a routine and should be a bottom-up more than a top-down process, treating field staff time as a scarce resource.

3. supervision should include evaluating work which has been done and joint planning of work to be done.

4. reporting should be kept high and streamlined and should include work done and problems encountered.

These assumed principles are selected from many. Other lists could have been drawn up. The crucial point is that these are relatively easy to put into practice and therefore a good point of entry in trying to sharpen the effectiveness of staff in the field. They are only a beginning; but they are probably a useful set to begin with.

There are many ways in which these principles can be put to work. With simpler procedures than those presented above, a supervisor can have a regular meeting with his field staff and discuss what they have been doing and what they should do, without requiring any paperwork at all. Or debriefing can be introduced simply by reading and discussing a daily diary. Reporting can be simplified and rationalized independently of any other change. But unless there is a minimal procedure, preferably formalized in some simple written record of agreement and plans, any routine of this sort is liable to lapse. The problem in applying these principles is to find the right level of complexity, the right amount of paperwork, the right connections between the parts. Needs are different in different situations and departments. Attention here has been on agricultural extension and to a lesser extent on community development. The work of other departments requires yet other patterns to be devised.

A potential application of this approach is in helping governments to achieve the equity objectives which are becoming increasingly prominent in official statements. In Eastern Africa the people in towns are generally better off than the people in the rural areas, but within the rural areas themselves there are brutal contrasts in levels of living: on the one hand progressive farmers, well established with cash crops, well connected with government services, with substantial cash incomes giving them means to invest in further land purchase, farm development, businesses, and their children's education; and on the other the so-called laggards, people with small plots of land, subsistence or sub-subsistence economies, many children, and negligible contact with the modern world. Short of revolutionary transformation any attempt to reach the latter is bedevilled by multiple difficulties which will not be overcome by any amount of rhetoric.

A major obstacle is the notorious tendency for extension workers, whether in agriculture, health, home economics or community development, to concentrate their attention on those who are already better off. For many years in many countries this was indeed official policy in agriculture. The Pupil and Master Farmers of Lesotho and Botswana, the Progressive Farmers of Uganda, and their equivalents elsewhere were deliberately sought out as innovators who would lead the way by setting an example to others. Since it is now fashionable to decry this approach, let it be said that it served a purpose; it was necessary to start somewhere; and where, as in Botswana, there was a critical threshold of capital in achieving viability in arable agriculture, it may have been particularly justified. But it did tend to widen the gap between the "progressive" farmers and the rest. Moreover, it legitimated what the extension worker was anyway inclined to do: to associate with and reciprocate services with those who were better off, who were more prepared to adopt new practices, who had resources and power and who could bestow benefits. Sometimes indeed as reported for veterinary services in one part of Kenya (Personal communication, David K. Leonard), the local rich and powerful received services free, whereas the poorer men were made to pay for them. It has to be recognised that the point of departure, in seeking to get through to and help those who are worse off, is one in which extension workers are powerfully locked in socially and economically with those who are already better off, and in which it is in their interests to provide them with services. "To him who hath shall be given . . .". It is also professionally natural for them to concentrate on those who have cash crops, if it is only for cash crops that they have advice or services to offer. They also often need to have a number of docile good farmers who are prepared to allow demonstrations on their farms, and to be on show to visiting dignitaries and even entertain them by slaughtering a beast. The extension worker is caught in an administrative, social and economic network in which he trades his resources (loans, subsidized equipment, privileged access to inputs, information) for reciprocal benefits which he is most likely to secure from the richer members of the community.

But the situation is indeed even more difficult than this. The extension workers may be largely invisible to senior officials; but worse, the poorer people are almost invisible to the extension workers. It is not just that they neglect them; they do not see them. When agricultural extension workers in Vihiga in Kenya carried out a survey (Moock, 1971) of a random sample of farmers in the areas where they worked, not only did they complain that the sample included far too few progressive farmers to be representative, but they were surprised and startled by the many poor people whom they were forced to visit. One Home Economics Assistant said that she burst into tears at the poverty and misery of some of the people in her sample, people whom in the course of her normal work she would never have met. These were the families of the invisible farmers, people rarely or never visited by extension workers, who rarely went to barazas, who lived largely out of contact with the modern world, and who were identified as a substantial minority in the three densely populated and economically advanced SRDP areas (Vihiga, Tetu and Irianyi) which were surveyed in the early 1970's (see Moock 1971 for Vihiga; Ascroft, Röling, Kariuki and Chege 1972 for Tetu; Ascroft, Barnes and Garst 1971 for Irianyi). The management problem is one of getting dispersed field workers to perceive and work with poor, low status farmers whom they are inclined to ignore. These farmers have a low capacity for demanding services, negligible sanctions to exercise if they do not receive them, and little or nothing to offer in exchange; and they are often caught in a trap of little land, poverty, ill-health, large families and apathy.

That it is no easy task to reach such people is shown by the experience of an imaginative and important SRDP experiment carried out in Tetu Division in Kenya, (Ascroft, Röling, Kariuki and Chege, 1973). The intention was to recruit for a special farmer training course only farmers who (i) had no grade cattle and (ii) had not adopted hybrid maize. These criteria were explained to subchiefs and junior agricultural staff who then selected the farmers. Those chosen were, it is true, laggards in one sense, that fewer of them than average for the area had previously been to farmers' training courses; but 15 per cent had already adopted hybrid maize, and no less than 68 per cent had grade cattle (*ibid*: 63). The authors honestly concluded that "the participants (were) considerably above average for progressiveness and . . . the courses have again helped those who need help least. Thus the experiment failed in reaching one of its important objectives: to reach below-average farmers." But one of the main achievements of the experiment was to identify and expose this difficulty, and to force the would-be reformer to face the conclusion which the experimenters drew, that "one cannot rely on local officials to select below-average farmers, probably because they do not know them" (*ibid:* 66—68).

The challenge then is to develop a repertoire of programmes and management techniques which will overcome these twists and knots which pervert the intention to reach those who are worse off. There are, of course, many measures for helping the rural sector as against the urban; but almost invariably those favour the better-off rural inhabitants while leaving the worse-off untouched. There are only a few measures that can help those who are worse off which are not intensive in their demands on field staff; among them is the sale of inputs in small packages which the small man may better be able to afford (Chege 1971). But most measures involve some direct contact between extension worker and farmer. The ILO Mission to Kenya argued for target minimum incomes (1972:316—318) and stated that the agricultural extension service should redirect its efforts to achieve "much more effective and widespread contact with the bulk of the farmers." (*Ibid.* 155) The question is how.

A short list of possible methods, drawing heavily on the SRDP experience and the ideas of Chege and Roling is:

(i) greater emphasis on extension to groups. This is widely recommended (for example Mbithi 1973; ILO Mission 1972:153). It conforms with the Leonard Principle of being easy to supervise and inspect. It is likely to reach down the range of farmers towards those who are less well-off.

(ii) mobilizing farmer demand for extension services. One unanticipated effect of issuing farm visit books in Mbere was that farmers demanded them from extension agents, forcing them into contact, and lengthening the lists of farmers recorded in the register as having been visited. A political drive could strengthen this tendency.

(iii) registers of farmers which show the frequency of visits (for an ingenious proposal with a dramatic visual effect, see Röling and Chege 1972:3—4) and which can be inspected by the extension worker and his supervisor to see how well he is spreading his attention.

(iv) farmer training for farmers in the less progressive categories, as pioneered in the Tetu SRDP with selection carried out by a senior officer as well as by local staff (Ascroft, Röling, Kariuki and Chege 1973).

(v) phasing out services to farmers and concentrating attention on those who are at an adoption or capital threshold, using farmer visit records and reporting systems which emphasize numbers who cross the threshold and who are then increasingly left on their own (Chambers and Feldman 1973:89—91, 235—243).

Using these or other methods, or a selection of them, a set of specially tailored work programmes can be drawn up using procedural approaches similar to those outlined above and designed to encourage, push and pull field staff into the behaviour which is required for the effective implementation of equity programmes.

The most critical question is, however, not whether such management systems can be devised, but whether there is the political and professional will to use them in these ways. Whatever the political pronouncements in past and forthcoming national plans, whatever the official rhetoric about equity, no major redirection of extension activity is likely to achieve lasting success without sustained political support. It may indeed be through a transformational approach in which the poorer people are given special treatment in special geographical areas

—*ujamaa* villages in Tanzania, Harambee settlement schemes in Kenya —that equity objectives in rural areas can most easily be attempted on any scale. But even if these approaches are pursued and are successful (and both rely on a diminishing stock of spare land) there will remain pockets of poverty in rural areas to which services can and should be directed. For this to be done, there must be further R and D (research and development) work on procedures which are tested and developed in field situations, with training for top and middle-level staff in management and in the operation of the procedures, and with sustained professional support from senior government staff. In agriculture this support may not be readily forthcoming, since the bias of professional education and training is towards the more complex aspects of farming and farm management, creating skills which can best be exercised with the more progressive farmers. Staff are, in fact, trained away from the poorer farmers, and further conventional training of staff is liable to mean an even stronger behavioural bias towards those who are already better off. We are driven, thus, to the conclusion, that for any major campaign effectively to reach those who are worse-off, it is not enough only to innovate with low-level management systems, essential though that is. It is necessary also to achieve a re-orientation of political and professional thinking and for this to be translated into training and into political and professional support. Only if that reorientation occurs will it be possible on any scale and over any length of time for the invisible men of field extension to be directed, persuaded and encouraged to reach and help the invisible and disadvantaged people who most need their services and advice.

IV. Managing Local Participation: Rhetoric and Reality

> ... Citizens of this land, through various development or planning committees at various levels, participated significantly in preparing the Second National Development Plan. It was a typical example of participatory democracy ... The Plan is a people's plan. It was designed and formulated by the people for their own development ...
>
>> Introduction to the Zambian Second National Development Plan 1972—1976, (Republic of Zambia 1971:v)

> There is a plan being drawn up now for this area. As soon as it is out, we will let you know what you are expected to do.
>
>> A Locational Agricultural Assistant in a public meeting in Migori Division, Kenya (reported by Oyugi 1973:7)

1. Definitions and perspective

Rhetoric has important political functions and relies on the loose use of words with ideological overtones. There is some justification for the vague use by political leaders of phrases like "self-reliance", "participatory democracy", and "local participation" in order to secure support and action; but there is less justification for the imprecise use of these phrases by academics and civil servants, since for them such usage may cover up bad or lazy thinking. For purposes of analysis and prescription it is best first to clarify the senses in which phrases are used and then to appraise the relationship between those senses and the reality. When this is done a wide gap may be found. This chapter seeks to clarify some of the issues involved and to suggest means whereby the gap between rhetoric and reality might be narrowed. It draws heavily on comparative experience with "local participation" in the countries of Eastern Africa, and much less than Chapters 2 and 3 on the SRDP in Kenya, since procedures for local participation were less developed and tested in the SRDP up to the end of 1972 than those for programming, implementation and field staff management.

Local participation can conveniently be analyzed in three ways: who participates; what institutions are involved; and what objectives and functions it has.

First, those who participate may be government staff at the local level, the local inhabitants of an area, or a combination of these two. The issue is complicated by the tendency for those government staff who originate in the area in which they work to think and act as local inhabitants (Oyugi 1973:10). A distinction can be made between (i) "participation by staff", meaning by those staff who typically do not originate in the area and who are liable to transfers out of it, (ii) "participation by the people", including both inhabitants and those staff who originate in the area, and (iii) "joint participation" in which both groups—outside staff and local inhabitants—are involved. But in practice the interaction of the two groups is complex and variable. District Development Committees, for example, may or may not include local inhabitants. This means that to use "local participation" in either the first or second sense would involve hair-splitting and make it difficult to describe the experience with those committees. To avoid such difficulties and also to include the range of meanings in common usage, "local participation" in this chapter is used to include all three categories—participation by staff, participation by the people, and joint participation by both staff and people.

Second, local participation can be analyzed in terms of the institutions through which it occurs. In Eastern Africa over the past decade these have included local government authorities, development committees, community development committees, self-help groups, public meetings, and local interest groups such as churches, women's groups and political parties. The institutions through which local participation occurs provide the most convenient categories for discussing experience, lessons and prescriptions and some of them will be used below.

Third, local participation can be analysed in terms of objectives and functions. The values ascribed to it in its various forms include:

- making known local wishes
- generating developmental ideas
- providing local knowledge
- testing proposals for feasibility and improving them
- increasing the capability of communities to handle their affairs and to control and exploit their environment
- demonstrating support for a regime

- doing what government requires to be done
- extracting, developing, and investing local resources (labour, finance, managerial skills, etc.)
- promoting desirable relationships between people, especially through co-operative work.

In Eastern Africa both the participation sought by governments and the institutions through which attempts have been made to achieve it have changed remarkably over the past fifty years. An historical perspective makes it easier to see the nature of the stage reached and what may be the most important current priorities. In the early colonial period the local participation sought by governments was rather limited and negative: the handling by surviving or artificial indigenous authorities of many matters which could be described as traditional; and the payment of taxes and the provision of labour. In the later colonial period, however, there was increasing attention to the development of local government institutions, mainly at the district level. Attempts were made to promote their growth as democratic elected bodies responsible for a wide range of local services including education, roads, health, markets, community development, and licensing plots and businesses. The experience with this phase, which reached its zenith in most countries around the time of independence, has been well documented in many articles in the Journal of Administration Overseas. In Kenya, Tanzania and Zambia, and to a lesser extent Uganda and Botswana, there were innumerable difficulties over supervision, staffing, staff training, revenue collection, technical services, payment of staff, an overemphasis on educational and health services to the neglect of others, corruption, and low calibre councillors lacking a sense of civic responsibility. These and other problems bedevilled rural local authorities and at worst almost paralyzed them. Kenya responded in 1969 by removing from District Councils the three most important services—roads, health and education—and transferring them to central government agencies operating in the districts. Much the same occurred in Tanzania. Elsewhere except perhaps in Botswana the trend has also been towards a reduction in local government responsibilities. Elected councillors consequently have less power than before; council staff have less prestige; and budgets are often dramatically smaller. Except in Botswana, local authorities are no longer seen, for the time being, as major vehicles for developing participation by local people.

In some countries, most clearly in Kenya, the rise and decline of local government occurred in parallel with the rise and decline in political parties and their local-level organisations. In this respect Tanzania is exceptional in the continuing vitality of the party at the lower levels. There may be a danger in treating Kenya as a paradigm in making comparisons. But it may be quite generally the case, elsewhere as in Kenya, that the failures of local government and the weakness of the party in representing and giving meaning to local aspirations have coincided with the growth and vigour of self-help groups. Lacking any other effective and reliable means of getting what they want, clans, churches and other groupings have identified themselves, organized, worked and competed for government and other external resources. The latest development in Kenya, where the urban elite, at high cost to themselves in money and time, have been promoting Institutes of Technology (Godfrey and Mutiso 1973) appears to represent the most advanced manifestation of this "unofficial" competition for resources, prestige and legitimacy, but now on a wider regional and ethnic instead of a narrower clan or religious basis. Like the earlier self-help projects in which secondary schools and health centres were put up all over the country, often without staffing or other recurrent resources, these latest institutes conflict with rational planning by some strictly economic criteria. But like the earlier schools and health centres, they are likely to be built for they represent the sublimation of powerful drives which, if frustrated, might find other outlets which would threaten political stability.

Meanwhile there has been a resurgence in the authority and discretion of government staff at regional or provincial and district levels. Partly this has been a function of time and experience: with independence, the District Governors in Zambia, the Area Commissioners in Tanzania, the District Commissioners in Kenya, and their counterparts elsewhere were thrown in at the deep end; but by the early 1970's most of them had gained substantial experience and considerable confidence in their ability to handle their jobs. The District Development Committees of which they were chairmen, and their equivalents at Provincial and Regional level, grew in influence, aided by block grants made to them for development purposes, and were sometimes involved in compiling and presenting development plans to ministries in the centre. The bold decentralization to the regions in Tanzania, including as it did the devolution of some budgetary powers and the posting of many civil servants from Dar es Salaam to the regions, seemed in 1973 likely further to enhance the authority, discretion and initiative of government staff at regional and district level; and Zambia was beginning to implement a similar reform (proposed in Republic of Zambia 1972). Even in Kenya, which had set its face against decentralization, a move towards district planning in 1973 suggested that the district level might continue to grow in importance.

It is difficult to generalize across countries. There are examples, like local government in Botswana, which appear to move against the trend. But in general in the early 1970's the position was this: representative local government had declined in powers and services; political parties had weakened, except in Tanzania; people had organized themselves into local groups to achieve what they wanted; and central government staff at local levels were more competent, confident and active than before. These trends suggest that the most important relationships to examine are those between the points of growth and dynamism: in particular between local interest groups and leaders on the one hand and government organizations and civil servants on the other. If relatively little is said in what follows about local government or about political parties, this does not mean that they are not sometimes important. It does, however, reflect their relative decline as institutions through which development decisions are made and resources allocated; for these now fall much more to the interest groups, to the civil servants and to those of the local elite who mediate between the two.

Local participation can be analyzed in terms of two streams of initiatives, communication and resources: those which are top-down, originating in government headquarters and penetrating towards and into the rural areas; and those which are bottom-up, originating among the people in the rural areas and directed upwards into the government machine. Given our concern here with government organization and local interest groups, the two most notable and important top-down initiatives in Eastern Africa have been development committees and block grants; and the most important bottom-up initiatives have been self-help projects. The experience with these will be considered in turn.

2. The experience with development committees

In the mid-1960's the participation of local-level staff and political leaders in discussing local development matters was widely sought through the formation of development committees at provincial/regional and district levels. In their early composition, style and operation they fall into two groups: large political forums; and smaller caucuses of civil servants. Each had its pathological extremes; and each its limited successes.

The large political forums are represented by Tanzania and Zambia. Having relatively vigorous political parties and politically appointed heads at provincial/regional and district levels, it was to be expected that Tanzanian and Zambian development committees would include substantial local political representation. In Tanzania the Regional Development Committees and the District Development and Planning Committees were presided over by political appointees, the Regional Commissioner and the Area Commissioner respectively. In Zambia, the Provincial Development Committees and District Development Committees were similarly presided over by the Minister of State (later, in 1969, the Provincial Cabinet Minister) and the District Governor respectively. In both countries there was considerable representation of the party on the committees, together with civil servants. Membership and attendances were large; Collins reported (1970:14) 40 to 50 participants in the Mwanza Regional Development Committee in Tanzania, and the figure for Kilimanjaro was higher; while in Zambia attendances were in the range of 40 to 100 or more (Tordoff 1968a: 429; Rainford 1971:180; Republic of Zambia 1972:89). Attendance tended to be cumulative. In one meeting a complaint was lodged about postal services. The town postmaster was invited to the following meeting to answer it. Thereafter he always received minutes and attended. The resulting elephantiasis burgeoned into small parliaments which lacked either procedures or an executive secretariat.

At best, meetings were dominated by a strong chairman; at worst they echoed with hollow rhetoric. On the positive side, they sometimes kept civil servants on their toes, especially where as in Zambia they were required to present progress reports and submit themselves to cross-questioning on the work of their departments (Rainford 1971: 189). They also provided a learning process for local political leaders regarding the problems, constraints and capabilities of the civil service departments. They did also succeed in creating something of a political forum for the expression of local opinions, for the proving of local politicians, and for the dissemination of some elements of national policy and political philosophy.

But the negative aspects of these bodies were formidable. Their style and value was highly sensitive to the personality of the chairman:

where he was authoritarian, they did little more than provide him with a platform. As membership grew, meetings flowed over into second and even third days, much to the irritation of civil servants and with a profligate cost in their time, particularly when any one civil servant was likely to be directly concerned with only a small part of the business discussed. Meetings were too big for technical discussion of the detail of projects. There were no formal procedures for making decisions and difficulty after a discussion in knowing what conclusion had been reached. As Collins pointed out for Tanzania (1970:17) ongoing programmes could be disrupted through changes in political decisions. Moreover in neither Tanzania nor Zambia did the development committees have any substantial formal executive authority. It is not surprising that they gradually came to be regarded as of doubtful utility and that in both countries reform was sought. An admirable summary of the negative aspects of the Zambian experience, much of which also applies to Tanzania, is given in the Simmance Report describing the Zambia Provincial Development Committee

The Committee meets quarterly, controls no funds, has no executive authority, and its membership is at the Cabinet Minister's discretion. It is probably fair to say that, in practice, it has passed beyond his control. No one knows any longer exactly who the members are. Council chambers (and their size is hardly modest) are becoming too small for the swelling concourse that attends. Membership varies but can be 100 or even more; one provincial head told us that he had to prepare 130 copies of papers for committee circulation. In another province, we were told with pride that the Minister had succeeded in reducing the membership from eighty six to fifty four. We do not decry this achievement but the figure still remains too large. The Provincial Development Committee has become more like a regional assembly. It is referred to freely as a "talking shop", "a training ground for politicians", and even, in the words of one Permanent Secretary, a "toothless bulldog".

(Republic of Zambia 1972:89)

In contrast to these large political forums, predominantly civil service committees were set up in those countries which had a civil servant as the senior representative of government at the provincial and district levels. The Provincial Development Committees of Kenya, the District Development Committees of Botswana and Kenya, and the District Team and Planning Committees of Uganda were chaired by Provincial and District Commissioners respectively. The chairman, secretary and treasurer of the local authority, where there was one, were usually members or were invited, but not usually Members of Parliament nor party officials. Local residents who were either influential or much involved in development work sometimes attended, as did organizers of the brigades in Botswana, and senior traders and businessmen elsewhere. Memberships of the committees were much smaller than those of the political forums and attendances at meetings were usually within the range of 10 to 25. Discussion was more technical and meetings rarely took more than one day.

These civil service development committees also contrasted with the political forums in their pathology. In their early years their meetings were often irregular and even rare. Rapid staff transfers impeded sensible and knowledgeable discussion of local development matters. One District Development Committee in Kenya met for the first time for a year in order to discuss proposals for a land use plan for the district; but of the district departmental heads present only one had been in the district when the previous meeting had been held, all the others having less than a year's local experience. The price of lack of local knowledge was a very high one to pay for whatever advantages stemmed from the small size of the committee and its predominantly civil service membership. Indeed, that membership had its own costs since when committees did meet they sometimes considered the collective interests of the members rather than district development. Welch has noted that one District Team and Planning Committee in Uganda spent much of its time "discussing topics that will solely benefit the District Team members themselves" (1969:218), including the price of food, the poor quality of fresh milk, the high price of petrol, the inadequacy of the up-country living allowance, the absence of price control in the district, and the need for a television station (ibid. 218—9). Welch concludes that "This over-concern with creature comforts of the Civil Service shown by the District Team, while being understandable, is nonetheless indicative of the Team's total unawareness of the major problems of the District" (ibid. 219). Such tendencies may have been more marked in the remoter districts. But they do illustrate the extreme situations which sometimes prevailed in the earlier years of civil service committees in which they either did not meet, or if they did meet, discussed their own grievances, constituting not a development committee but a civil service interest group.

It would be facile to lay the blame for this situation only at the door of the civil servants. To be sure, more initiative could have been shown. But generally, the response was a rational one, given an undefined situation in which it was by no means certain that initiative would be rewarded. For Uganda, Kirunda has summed up the situation:

... the attitude of many members of the District Team and Planning Committee (DTPC) in Uganda that the DTPC is useless, has, as it were, killed the DTPCs ... if you read the minutes of these teams from any one of the districts in the country, you will not fail to see that either members are not keen on meetings of these Planning Committees, or that items that are so irrelevant to any planning are discussed, or that the members themselves are often asking their Chairman (the DC) or people from the Ministry of Planning and Economic Development what their role is and whether their existence as Planning Committees is really necessary.

(1971:17)

For Kenya, Gertzel has shown that during their first two years the development committees failed to put down roots. In many districts meetings were held only on the occasion of a visit by the Minister of Economic Planning, his Assistant Minister, or his officials. There was no regular reporting back from the committees to the Ministry (1970: 10). In the words of the Ndegwa Commission one of the reasons for the shortcoming of the committees was that "the actual duties and responsibilities of all the members of these committees, and the routines to be followed in plan-implementation, progress-reporting and plan-revision at the District level were never defined" (Republic of Kenya 1971a:115). The Simmance Report makes a similar diagnosis for Zambia (Republic of Zambia 1972:90). Other explanations are also valid supplements: the early lack of professional planning staff outside capital cities was certainly a factor. But the most persuasive explanation of failures of committees to meet and of non-developmental or vague discussions when they did meet is that they had not been given anything to do. Once again the evidence leads to the conclusion that field staff were underutilized and that the key to unlocking and exploiting their resources lay with the design and introduction of procedures.

This interpretation is amply borne out by the evidence of activity when committees were given clear guidelines or asked to recommend on development decisions. The SRDP experience may be taken as one example. When it appeared that there was a good chance that plans prepared at district level with assistance from above might receive funds, District Development Committees (DDCs) were galvanized into unwonted action, holding much more frequent meetings, and with the members contributing ideas and proposals. Elsewhere in Kenya, when

92

DDCs were asked to recommend on priorities for road maintenance, for new roads, and for rural water supplies, their meetings achieved a vital and responsible focus. But in both these examples, the initiative in requesting advice and decision had to come from outside. A prior condition for the effective working of the committees was a capability higher in the government machine to set guidelines and make requests for action which the government machine could then handle. Such a capability takes time to develop. An overhasty approach quickly leads to disillusion at the local level, as has so often happened when shopping list plans have been requested by the centre. As with other institutions, so with development committees, growth has to be gradual and organic, and demands related to capacity.

In their changes over time most of these committees have shown an interesting tendency to converge on a common pattern. The experience in Kenya is one example. At first in the mid-1960's two parallel committees were intended at both provincial and district levels—development committees of civil servants, and development advisory committees including Members of Parliament (MPs) and other local representatives. In practice the advisory committees were resented by the civil servants and rarely called; and sometimes when meetings were called, the dates were arranged to coincide with parliamentary sittings in Nairobi so that the MPs would find it difficult to attend. In one Province, however, (Nyanza) a determined attempt was made both to give responsibilities to development committees at district level and to secure the participation of MPs. The result was that the committees functioned regularly and well, and although MPs' attendances were still erratic compared with those of civil servants, the experience was sufficiently positive for the pattern to be adopted nationally. The resulting committees, including civil service departmental heads, local authority officials and chairmen, and a few prominent local citizens by co-option, was paralleled in the recommendations of the Simmance Report in Zambia (Republic of Zambia 1972:93—5) and by the development committees in Tanzania, although in all cases there were local variations, most notably in the relationships of these committees to local authorities. The resulting bodies, with memberships and attendances likely to be in the range of 20—40, do however appear large for committee deliberations; and a pattern of smaller executive committees is desirable and sometimes exists. The recurring puzzle is how to balance representation—requiring more members, with useful discussion—requiring fewer.

The most obvious conclusions to draw from the experience with development committees are:

- committees function best when they are given definite and realistic developmental tasks. Without these, they become either talking shops or self-centred interest groups. The capacity, higher in government, to work out and devolve responsibilities is a precondition for effective functioning.
- size is critical: once committees get over about 20 in attendance, speeches replace the easier exchanges typical of committees, the more timid members keep quiet, those (usually politicians) who are more used to large audiences dominate proceedings and meetings take a long time and are inconclusive.
- at this stage in most countries the best system appears to be that which is developing, of two types of body: larger policy-oriented development committees of politicians and civil servants; and smaller action-oriented executive committees mainly or entirely of civil servants.

3. The experience with block grants

The most widespread and obvious developmental task that has been given to development committees has been responsibility for managing block grants for development purposes. These grants have been of two types.

First, departments of community development have been allocated modest sums which they have disbursed through a variety of local committees in order to assist self-help projects. In Botswana, such funds have been made available by the Botswana Christian Council, the American Embassy, and other sources, and allocated by a central committee in the capital meeting fortnightly and processing applications received from District Development Committees. In Kenya, a hierarchy of community development committees has existed to varying degrees and has to varying degrees been "captured" by Provincial and District Development Committees. In Tanzania, what were known as Community Development Trust Funds were used to assist self-help projects (Makoni 1969:8). It is dangerous to generalize from sketchy evidence, but while all these various funds were small, they undoubtedly did get through to the lower levels of administration, although in their allocation there was probably a general preference for larger rather than smaller self-help projects.

The second type of block grant was more substantial, more controversial and more interesting. Block grants became policy in Zambia in 1966 (Republic of Zambia, 1972:87—88), in Tanzania in 1967 (Collins 1970:6), in Uganda in 1969 (Kirunda 1971:2) and in Kenya in 1971. The experience in these four countries makes for lively contrasts and comparisons with important lessons.

In Zambia the block vote was as called the Bottleneck Fund. It was a lump sum of money to be given to each Provincial Development Committee (PDC) "to enable it to overcome unforeseen bottlenecks in the execution of approved programmes of development that either are not the responsibility of any single Ministry or cannot be easily solved by normal procedures or through local authority action". (Republic of Zambia, 1972:87—88 quoting Republic of Zambia 1966:18). The sums involved were small, £25,000 (K50,000) for each province each year, amounting in total over the plan period to less than one per cent of the capital allocation for local as opposed to national projects (Republic of Zambia 1972:88). The formal rules did not allow the PDC any discretion in determining what constituted a bottleneck and all proposed expenditures had to be referred to Lusaka. However, PDCs exercised their ingenuity and indeed casuistry in interpreting the guidelines and in practice proposed to use and actually used the Fund to shortcut the long process of applying through normal channels for finance for a variety of purposes: departmental projects; undertakings such as beautifying a waterfall (in order to avoid losing the balance of the Fund at the end of the year); small capital and developmental projects; and purposes like building garages and hotels which did not remotely resemble the original intentions of the Fund and which exposed its use to charges of corruption (Rainford 1971). In consequence, the Fund was terminated in 1970 after three years of eventful use.

In Tanzania, the idea of the Regional Development Fund (RDF) (see Makoni 1969: Collins 1970) introduced in 1967 may have been borrowed from Zambia. The sums allocated to each region was at first the same—£25,000 (Shs.500,000) per annum; the Fund was to be used on the recommendation of the Regional Development Committee (RDC); and suballocations from it were subject to approval in Dar es Salaam. Thus far it was similar to the Bottleneck Vote. The RDF differed however, in having clearer and more manageable guidelines:

it was intended for small economic projects; allocations had to be for Shs.50,000 or less; and projects requiring supplementary recurrent expenditure were ruled out. Ideally, proposals were to be suggested by Village Development Committees and passed up through the District level to the RDC. In practice this was at first difficult or impossible, and proposals were taken off the shelf by technical officers, who seized the opportunity to implement projects which they cherished but for which they had not been able to obtain funds. A high proportion of the early projects were roads and bridges, imposing an unanticipated burden on certain technical services. Many of the first year's proposals were rejected in Dar es Salaam, the most common reasons given being lack of economic justification, being suitable for other financing, exceeding the Shs.50,000 limit, or benefitting individual farmers rather than the community (Makoni 1969:17). The experience, however, was generally positive, and in 1968 the RDF was doubled, to one million shillings per region. RDCs were given the final power of choice of RDF projects (Collins 1970:6—7 quoting Presidential Circular 1/68) though preference was to be given to projects involving communal production, and later *ujamaa* villages.

As so often with new initiatives in rural development, it was during its teething troubles that the RDF received most attention from researchers and evaluators. Although, as Makoni points out, evaluating the RDF in its first years would be like photographing a horserace with a poor camera, some points of evaluation can be made. On the negative side the better-off regions found it easier to spend the funds, accentuating inter-regional inequities. In some cases local notables or officials benefited from its use (Collins 1970:26, 41). It was difficult to generate good projects from the village level, and when they were generated there was a heavy elimination: in four districts studied by Makoni 121 projects were received by the DDC, which sent 66 to the RDC, which sent on only 26 of the original 121 to the Ministry of Local Government and Rural Development. The RDC may also have slowed rural development through the diversion of technical resources from projects where there were economies of scale (for example, large water projects) to projects which were smaller and where less could be achieved in terms of private benefits for the same scarce technical resources. But on the positive side it galvanized the RDCs into action and decision-making, forced government staff to think, placed major responsibility on the Regional Commissioner, acted as a training tool for district and regional staff, and enabled them to exercise initiative and learn on the job by having something positive to do and to be judged by.

In Uganda, the experience with the so-called Rural Development Programme in which £5,000 (Shs.100,000/—) was allocated by the Ministry of Finance to each parliamentary constituency for the financial year 1969/70 has been well documented by Kirunda for one district—Ankole—with six constituencies (1971). This exercise was as political as it was disastrous. The funds were at the discretion of a project committee of local politicians chaired by the Member of Parliament if he belonged to the ruling party. In constituencies where the Member was an independent or belonged to the banned Democratic Party, the chairman was some other MP of the ruling party. The official purposes were to involve the people in their own development, to secure savings through voluntary labour, and to meet the felt needs of the community. In fact, an election was imminent and it is difficult to imagine that the main motivation was anything other than the provision of powers of local patronage to the Members of Parliament of the ruling party. Civil servants were not members of the project committees. Four of the six committees in Ankole District submitted projects without consulting technical officers but all projects were approved by the responsible Committee of the Ministry of Finance. Public meetings were not held and the masses were not involved. Normal tender procedures for contracts were not followed. There was widespread corruption and an injunction to District Commissioners to exercise some degree of supervision came too late to do much more than place them in an acutely embarrassing position. Voluntary labour was difficult to mobilize and many of the projects were left unfinished or completed to a poor standard. Civil servants were as reluctant to help as the project committees were reluctant to ask them for help. The "pet political personality projects", as they were known to some in Ankole District, alienated the civil service and can have done little to secure support for the ruling party.

Kenya's approach was much more cautious. In the 1971/72 financial year K£100,000 was allocated equally between the seven provinces, each province receiving about W£14,000 and the average for a district being about K£2,500. The grants were intended to fill gaps in development and were regarded as a preliminary step towards district planning. Projects were to be put up by District Development Committees through the province and approved in Nairobi. The guidelines included that projects should not normally give rise to recurrent expenditure; should conform with the objectives of the national plan; and should be implementable with existing resources in the field. Priority was to be given to economic projects such as cattle dips, fish ponds, dam construction, afforestation, soil conservation, flood control and small road building. While it was early to evaluate the experience, the indications in early 1973 were that as elsewhere district-level officers had responded vigorously and with enthusiasm to the opportunity to exercise some discretion. It may be no coincidence that the most popular projects—cattle dips—required a careful mixture of local consultation, self-help, government inputs, and interdepartmental co-operation. Free funds of this sort, administered by development committees, can provide just the incentive and focus needed to bring together the various parties involved in a project, and their benefits may thus be greater where several departments and interest groups have to be involved. However, as had occurred earlier in Tanzania, the less advanced and less well staffed districts found it more difficult to spend their allocations and regional imbalances resulted. But the experience in Kenya was sufficiently positive for much larger grants to be considered: the ILO Mission went as far as to mention £40,000 per district per year (ILO 1972:321—2).

On the basis of the experiences with block votes in Zambia, Tanzania, Uganda and Kenya some judgements can be made. Zambia, the original innovator, made the initial error of setting such stringent conditions for the use of funds that the rules were broken by committees, the funds misallocated, and the block vote system discredited, so that the case for abandonment argued by the Ministry of Finance became difficult to oppose and the vote was stopped. Tanzania had looser criteria and more decentralized discretion at an early stage and found that trusting the Regional Development Committees to follow centrally-determined guidelines paid off not only in the projects which resulted but also in the experience gained by the officers concerned. Uganda made the obvious mistake of using the vote for political patronage and excluding the civil service, with disastrous results and a lost opportunity for developing the capability of its civil servants. Kenya was hypercautious in its reluctance to trust its very competent field staff, but found that a small block grant to districts was enthusiastically received by District Development Committees.

A most important lesson to be gleaned concerns the right balance between the sums involved, the discretion devolved, the level to which devolution takes place, and the capability that exists at that level. Large sums distort existing programmes and are liable to bias actual resource distribution to favour the better-off areas where the capacity to spend is better developed. Too little discretion encourages evasion and bending the rules at the local level, while too much encourages corruption. Devolution too far down the hierarchy leads to problems of control and reconciling proposals, while devolution only to provincial/ regional level may encourage a bias towards only the larger and more prestigious projects. The capability among government field staff effectively to handle block votes is, however, probably far greater than the cautious accountants of central treasuries are inclined to recognize; and in the absence of resources and discretion, much of that capability lies unexploited, a dormant national resource. In mobilizing that capability, careful use of block grants is a valuable and proven means.

In analyzing the evolution of development committees and the experience with block votes it is useful to examine changes over time. At any stage major weaknesses may be evident in any institution but it may be only through persevering, and especially through promoting staff development through the devolution of discretion, that future development can be assured. This is particularly vital with the top-down initiatives of government trying to reach and involve rural people. In the early stages they may not be reached. When the Regional Development Fund was introduced in Tanzania it largely failed in its intention of involving Village Development Committees in submitting projects. It penetrated and activated as far down as the District. The pressure of time and the lengthy processes of explanation and discussion needed to elicit acceptable projects from village level combined to prevent full consultation (Makoni 1969 *passim*). Similarly, the first round of planning with the Special Rural Development Programme in Kenya was not able to include consultation to determine the wishes of local inhabitants: had it done so, there would probably have been such delays that the SRDP would never have started. But these were only stages. With the experience gained and the gathering capacity to act resulting from the experience, it was possible for the RDF to penetrate lower later, and for the SRDP three years later to contemplate low-level locational seminars to suggest projects and programmes as part of a replan exercise. Moreover, had it not been for these earlier stages, later reforms and developments might have been unthinkable or impracticable. The major decentralization and reorganization undertaken by Tanzania in 1972 owed much to the earlier experience with the RDF; had regional officers not already shown their capacity for responsible fund allocations it would have been much harder to accept the idea of regional budgets. Had the SRDP not helped to demonstrate the capacity of development committees and local-level staff to contribute ideas and prepare plans, district planning in Kenya would probably have been even slower in starting than it was (it had been recommended by the Ndegwa Commission in 1971 [Republic of Kenya 1971: Chapter 12] but little had been done by early 1973). The direction of change is, however, at least as important as its speed. In Kenya, Tanzania, and Zambia the trend in 1973 was unmistakably towards greater discretion and control for the local-level officers of central government.

Increases in authority and discretion for government staff at local levels is sometimes confused with participation by the people; but it is by no means the same thing. Development committees and block grants at regional/provincial and district level increase participation by staff and often by certain of the locally-based elite. Such participation may or may not be used to increase the discretion and autonomy of people lower in the scale, both staff and local inhabitants. Whether it is so used depends on how local aspirations and official resources are mixed. The extent of participation by the people associated with or resulting from the top-down approach represented by development committees and block grants depends partly on development committee composition but much more on the procedures which govern their operation, the resources of which they dispose, the strength and nature of popular demands, and the local institutions and interest groups through which they are articulated.

4. Managing self-help

The vigour, nature and geographical density of self-help projects varies between countries, within countries, and in any one area over time. There are places where a community development effort is needed to help people to see what they need; there are other places where an explosion of enthusiasm has created a chaotic proliferation of projects. There are situations (as in parts of Kenya in 1973) in which self-help groups wish to hide, to avoid political or administrative support which might distort or unreasonably expand their projects (Almy and Mbithi 1972), and at the other pole, there are self-help groups with extremely dependent attitudes which have formed themselves only as a device for securing resources. There are also sharp contrasts between countries: Zambia has been cursed with ample government resources which have stunted local self-help by making it rational for people not to help themselves but to petition for help; Kenya, at the other extreme, may be exceptional in the extraordinary energy and diversity of the Harambee movement, with its roots in the long struggle for independence (Anderson 1971) and its highly competitive local character. Since Kenya's self-help is the best documented (Anderson 1971; Holmquist 1970; Mbithi 1972; Mbithi and Almy 1972; Mutiso and Godfrey 1973; Oyugi 1973) most of the discussion which follows is derived from Kenyan experience. Nonetheless many of the opportunities and problems elsewhere in Eastern Africa seem to be similar to, if less intense than, those in Kenya; and the measures which work or seem workable in Kenya may also work elsewhere.

Self-help presents major opportunities for development. The extractionist view—that it enables the exploitation of resources which would otherwise lie dormant, that it saves government funds, that it makes use of underutilized labour, that it releases pressure on overextended government agencies—is valid as far as it goes. But self-help also has other values. It can increase the competence and confidence of a group and its members in handling their affairs. The example of the so-called *mabati* groups of women in Kenya indicates how one success can lead on to another: for having begun by working together to raise funds to put iron (*mabati*) roofs on their members' houses, they moved on to buying grade cattle, fencing dips, building better kitchens, and demanding the services of community development, health, veterinary and home economics staff. Again, where a capital asset is put up—schools being the most common example—continuing management is much more likely to be successful where there is a group and personal commitment through past contributions and sacrifices made. There is also a political gain in the sense of change and achievement which flows from self-help. A major value, in Kenya at least, has been the barrage of demands directed by self-help groups to civil servants, particularly in community development (Edward 1969: *passim*) which, although sometimes distracting, keeps them on their toes. In ways such as these in most countries of Eastern Africa, self-help initiatives have made major contributions to national development.

The management of self-help projects, seen primarily from a top-down government point of view, has, however, presented huge problems, a nightmare for planners, a headache for administrators, and a wobbly plinth for politicians. These problems can be considered under four headings: control and planning; authoritarianism; implementation; and operation and maintenance.

First, control and planning problems have received the most attention, being the most monumentally conspicuous. Self-help groups often form to construct buildings designed for the provision of services. The long-term objective is usually that the government should provide the service to the local community—most notably schools and health services in the 1960's. But the resources required—government funds, contributions from the elite, and most important of all, high-level approval for staffing and recurrent expenditure—are scarce and difficult to secure. For these scarce resources, the clans, religious groups, clusters of population and other interest groups which take part in self-help compete with one another. The main focus of the competition is the construction of a building. This lends itself to self-help activity through contributions in labour and in kind and through the visibility of achievement; but at least as important, the building constitutes a powerful bid in the competition. As Holmquist has well said, self-help projects are pre-emptive (1970:222). If there can be only one health centre in a locality, the group that constructs the first and best building for it may stand the best chance of securing it for their sublocality. The strategy is risky but understandable.

The results are, however, often unfortunate. Examples are legion and well known: two dips built by rival clans within a few yards of one another; two secondary schools, one empty, the other with only a few pupils, a mile or two apart; shells of buildings which have never been completed, or if completed, never used; poorly staffed schools; dispensaries in low priority areas while higher priority areas lack health facilities; technical considerations ignored, as in the classic case in Kisii District in Kenya where technical rationality in a dips programme required a steady spread of dips to expand the frontier of a disease-free zone but where the self-help groups were scattered and moved at different speeds (Holmquist 1970). The outcomes have been not only unsystematic development, heavy strains on government resources and often disillusion at the local level, but also more positively the expression of popular wants which political parties, local authorities and civil servants were unable or unwilling to carry. The gradual legitimation of Harambee secondary schools in Kenya and their progressive incorporation into the official educational system is an example of a powerful grassroots movement forcing the government's hand, of the tail wagging the dog.

A second problem is the authoritarian style of much of the mobilization for self-help, at least in Kenya. In several respects administrative officers are political leaders and concerned with their legitimacy and acceptance by the people. Lacking other meaningful developmental roles, they have devoted attention to stimulating and supporting self-help, but they have naturally brought to this task the style and techniques of other aspects of their work. There is a tendency for communication in barazas to be one-way, from the District Officer or the Chief to the people (Nyangira 1970). Moreover, so-called voluntary contributions of labour may cover a wide range of practices, from forced labour with a legally enforceable penalty for default, to work in a group voluntarily joined without pressure. Whenever there is administrative pressure for labour turnouts, then the forced nature is likely to be more pronounced. It is, however, in contributions of cash or kind that the totalitarian character of some self-help is most noticeable. Administrative officers, chiefs and subchiefs transfer easily the style and methods for collecting tax to collecting for self-help. Nyangira reports that those who refused to contribute to a Harambee Secondary School in Western Kenya had one sheep or goat per head of household confiscated and auctioned, the proceeds going towards the project (1970:10). An administrative reflex has been applied to self-help, and this is by no means entirely bad; but it does change the view of self-help from a pure spontaneous voluntary movement to a semi-compulsory form of quasi-local government, in which contributions are exacted like any other tax, but with the advantage over conventional local authorities that the relation between contribution given and service received is clearer to the person taxed.

Third, there has been a wide range of problems in implementation. Where bids have been made for official resources, there have often been unconscionable delays: the request is sent upwards and sometimes lost forever in a bureaucratic maze; or returned after many months with requests for additional information; or accepted, but only after long enough has passed for local enthusiasm to have waned. (A notable exception was the handling of self-help fund requests in Botswana in 1972, with quick decisions made by a central committee which met every two weeks.) In other cases, the procedures to be followed and the path to be traced by a request are not known and time is wasted in chasing up blind alleys. Where official support is given, there may then be problems of phasing inputs. The cement arrives but sets in the rains because all able-bodied people are out planting their farms and cannot afford time for labour. A pipeline-laying crew arrives but the trenches for the waterpipe have not been dug, or not dug deeply enough. Technicians have their programmes to follow, and the local people also have theirs—critically important where subsistence cultivation is concerned; and these two often do not mesh. Or technical advice is not sought, or sought too late, or provided too late, or not provided at all. There may be interdepartmental problems in the official agencies: community development staff at loggerheads with the administration, a common condition based on mutual jealousy; or a technical department—water affairs, or veterinary services—wishing to employ direct labour to get a job done quickly, while community development and the administration prefer to mobilize the people to work. Or again, a certain level of local contribution in cash may be required and may be delayed, holding up and even disrupting a programme of work for officials. Some of these problems may sometimes be difficult to avoid; but many of them, on close inspection, relate to communication, perception and understanding between individuals and groups and should be remediable.

A fourth and neglected set of problems concerns the operation of completed projects. This is liable to be dismissed as a function of good initial control and planning: if the health centre had been "properly planned" then there would have been adequate staff and drugs to operate it. But in practice it is often not so simple. The group which built the dip did not realize that they would have to employ a dip attendant, would have to raise funds for the dip poison, would have to maintain the fence and would have to ensure the water supply. The group that built the school ignored the need for teachers' houses, the rising standards demanded by teachers, the need for a water supply, and so on. But perhaps it is right that these needs are not always clearly perceived in the early stages. They then later call forth the "creativity" of Hirschman's principle of the Hiding Hand (1967), according to which it is often only because people do not foresee difficulties that they launch out on projects and become committed to them; but faced later with unforeseen problems, they find they have a greater capacity or creativity for overcoming them than they thought. Whether such creativity is mustered depends critically on the degree of self-reliance of the self-help group. If it has been featherbedded with excessive outside help, it will be less likely effectively to manage the operation of the completed project than if it has made most of the initial effort itself.

Measures to tackle these problems tend to cut across some or all of them at once. Some of the principles and techniques described in chapters 2 and 3 apply also here, as do useful suggestions made by Almy and Mbithi (IDS 1972, appendix G) for participation by the people generally. Drawing on these and other sources, ten principles and measures can be put forward for managing self-help:

(i) *programming resource allocations:* Some of the confusion and delays in dealing with bids for resources can be overcome by the government staff concerned coming together and carrying out a programming exercise (see pp. 44—46) for the process of allocating funds and other resources to projects. In Kenya in 1972 this was undertaken in some SRDP areas and had the beneficial effects of forcing the fixing of dates of meetings and demonstrating the need for decisions to be speeded up and taken lower down the hierarchy.

(ii) *joint programming by government staff and self-help groups:* A legitimate criticism of the PIM programming of self-help has been that it has not involved the self-help groups or their leaders in setting targets and dates, and that therefore government staff might be driven to forceful and authoritarian methods in order to meet targets and deadlines for self-help contributions. This could be overcome for any one project through a meeting of self-help leaders, community development staff, a contractor if there is one, and any technical staff involved, to decide and agree who is going to do what, when and how. The procedure could be a discussion with a written record, or a blackboard could be used as in the programming exercise, depending on the literacy of the group. In the case of Botswana a system of monthly checks on progress and a district level meeting to decide any remedial action was recommended in 1972 (Chambers and Feldman 1973: 215—7).

(iii) *Procedures which "close" low down in the hierarchy:* Delays and difficulties can be reduced by giving more discretion lower down in the hierarchy. It should not be necessary, given competent staff and clear guidelines, for the provincial/regional level to have to approve allocations of self-help funds; it merely increases work at both district and provincial level. In some cases, discretion might even be devolved to subdistrict level.

(iv) *Rules of thumb for identifying types of project:* Different types of project often require different procedural treatment. The most useful classification of project types may be according to the support, if any, which they require. Categories can be based on what degrees and mixes of assistance in the form of capital, technical advice, technical support, recurrent costs and recurrent staffing are needed. Different types of project will then have different paths through the procedures.

(v) *Clear specification of phases and procedures for projects:* Much confusion arises from ignorance on the part of both people and staff of procedures to be followed, if indeed any have been worked out. Procedures can be related to phases in projects (planning, submission, approval, joint programming, construction, operation, etc.) which can be monitored, for example by a community development assistant or his equivalent using a simple bar chart.

(vi) *progress-reporting:* Self-help groups require to be kept informed of progress on the official side; equally staff need to know how self-help contributions of labour or cash or kind are progressing. Regular contact on a monthly basis combined with a progress report by the community development staff to the subdistrict or district level is normally not difficult to organize and can become part of a field staff management system. It encourages groups to know that their progress is assessed regularly; and it is good for staff to be forced by a procedure into making visits and keeping up to date.

(vii) *effective two-way communication:* It is obviously important for the people to know about government plans and priorities and about the procedures they should follow; it is equally important for staff to be in close touch with and sensitive to local aspirations, needs and ideas. Almy and Mbithi have good suggestions and point out the dangers of non-discussion and non-representation through the medium of meetings of leaders, senior representatives, and the higher level development committees. The levels and media of discussion are critical here. They write, of Kenya,

The sub-chief's baraza has usually been a forum for earnest discussion of plans and rectification of complaints, but the chief's baraza is usually addressed only by recognized local leaders and at the Divisional/District levels the only local participation is to sit in the hot sun and clap when visiting dignitaries have finished lecturing in a strange language.

(IDS: 1972:G9)

It is, perhaps, only at the very low levels that the full and open meeting is effective; and higher up there has to be resort to representation or selection of leaders and discussion in committee. The moral

106

would seem to be that government staff should try to penetrate down to the level at which such general meetings can be effective, and that above that level there should be a hierarchy of development committees including local opinion leaders and staff.

(viii) *administrative control and mediation:* Preventing bad self-help (bad siting, duplication, no staff, no funds, no recurrent resources, etc.) is likely to be an untidy and incomplete operation where self-help is vigorous, but a good upwards information system through community development or other staff, and good downwards communication of policies and guidelines may go a long way in discouraging poor initiatives. But the essence of self-help is that people identify a need for themselves and try to satisfy it; and launching out secretly on a "bad" project, or allowing several projects to go ahead, in the expectation that there will be a better chance of at least one of them being supported, is often rational behaviour on the part of would-be client groups or their leaders. As with other aspects of participation, we are concerned with establishing and maintaining balances in shifting situations according to conflicting criteria, especially "rational" planning against popular demand. The optimal situation will always be suboptimal from a planning point of view alone.

(ix) *avoiding top-down collection targetry:* The most damaging forms of extra-legal expropriation of property and extortion of funds that have taken place in the name of self-help have resulted from collection targets set at provincial or district level and then disaggregated down to chiefs and even sub-chiefs, with deadlines for delivery, reaching such unreasonable lengths that a subchief might resign over the issue, as in one case when the collection demanded was in a poor area suffering from drought in order to support a new service in a richer area. People, or at worst local leaders, should set their own collection targets, if targets there are to be. Administrative staff may perhaps reasonably be judged by their tax collections; they should not be judged by the extent to which they collect centrally determined sums of self-help contributions.

(x) *optimal levels of assistance:* Too much assistance can kill the spirit of self-reliance; too little may mean that a project is never undertaken or if undertaken never completed. Since several often conflicting factors and criteria govern the levels of assistance, simple prescriptions are liable to be misleading. But a few points which apply widely are:

- Where technical implementing capacity (water engineers and technicians, heavy road-making machinery and its skilled staff, etc.) are a critical bottleneck determining the rate of service installation, there is a case for abandoning self-help labour with its probable inefficiencies and delays

- unless their action requires recurrent support or is in some sense markedly antisocial, groups which wish to be independent of government or political support should be allowed to go their way
- outside support should provide what groups find it more difficult to provide for themselves
- outside support should not provide what groups find it easier to provide for themselves.

These injunctions may appear obvious common sense; if so, it is strange how often they are not followed.

5. Participation and equity

The way in which words are used in the rhetoric of self-reliance and participation encourages the idea that increased participation will mean a more democratic, egalitarian and equitable society. The idea that the participation advocated in plans and policy speeches reaches and benefits all the people is important for the reassurance of political leaders. There is just enough truth in this belief to sustain it; and it is reinforced by the highly selective experience of political leaders who are usually shown the best of everything, and who usually see that best on its best behaviour. But very often, and far more often than either political leaders or civil servants perceive or wish to perceive, participation means more influence and resources to those who are already influential and better off, while those who are less influential and less well off benefit much less, or do not benefit, or actually lose.

There are many ways in which "participation" accentuates inequity. Greater local participation in planning tends to widen regional inequalities. It favours those areas which are better able to produce plans and to implement them: the early experience with the Regional Development Fund in Tanzania was that the more prosperous regions (with the more competent staff, better infrastructure, better services) were more effective in spending the fund, while some of the remoter and more backward regions lagged and returned large sums unspent.

Participation in planning is also likely to mean plans drawn up either by civil servants or by civil servants together with a few members of the local elite. Participation in development committees can mean that those who are already well off approve projects and programmes which favour and support those who are already well off. Participation in self-help labour can mean that the women, already overworked, turn out while the men find excuses. Participation through "voluntary" contributions can mean an income-regressive flat rate tax which hits the poorest hardest; and failure to pay, as with contributions to some of Kenya's institutes of technology, may be penalized through the denial of public services—health treatment, the right to buy a bicycle licence, and so on—until a receipt for a minimum contribution can be shown. Participation in the local management of economic activities is even more incquitable. The privileges secured by the richer and more influential members of marketing co-operatives in Eastern Africa and elsewhere have been widely exposed. (Apthorpe 1972:81 ff; Widstrand ed. 1970; Widstrand ed. 1972; Worsley 1971; Saul 1973.) In pastoral societies measures for communal management of grazing and water resources have almost invariably benefited the larger stock-owners to the detriment of the smaller men: dam committees set up in Botswana to manage new dams charged a flat rate to all users, regardless of whether they brought hundreds of stock to water, or only one or two, in effect excluding the poorer people from the club; similarly when Council boreholes, which charged on a pro rata basis for numbers of stock watered, were handed over to local syndicate management, rates were changed to a flat rate for each stock owner regardless of the number of stock he watered. Again, it is notorious that land reform programmes, necessarily (short of a revolutionary situation) working through local committees, are captured by local elites who benefit more than the programme intends. In sum, all too often participation proclaimed on the platform becomes appropriation and privilege when translated into action in the field.

This should scarcely be surprising, except to those who, for ideological reasons or because they are simple-minded, or more commonly from a combination of these causes, reify "the people" and "participation" and push them beyond the reach of empirical analysis. The tendency for local elites to capture projects and programmes and use them for their own benefit should indeed be recognized as a fact of life. Moreover, there are benefits as well as costs in this. Leaders are often leaders because they have ability, and projects may be better managed through their participation. Leaders, especially where there is an active political party, may seek support and legitimacy and so have an incentive to spread the benefits of projects to more rather than fewer people. A conflict between the aims of good leadership and management on the one hand, and of distribution and equity on the other, is, however, likely to be a persistent feature which will remain difficult to overcome. Moreover, there are such variations between conditions in different areas that generalized prescriptions for participation and equity are more shaky and dangerous than in other more uniform contexts such as field staff management. All the same, six measures to mitigate the inequity which flows from participation and to improve its equity effects can be proposed.

First, in allocating support between alternative self-help projects, preference should be given to those to which all have access, or to which a wider rather than narrower band of the population will have access. A scale of desirability can be drawn up according to this criterion, with at one pole those projects which benefit all members of the community more or less equally—the village well, the health post (if treatment is free), the social hall—moving through those which benefit all but some much more than others—the access road, the nursery school, the primary school, the co-operative store—to those which only benefit a minority of the community or a few individuals who are already better of—the secondary school with high fees, the cash crop processing plant when only a few can grow the cash crop, the institute of technology to which only a few will be able to send their children.

Second, contributions to projects should be related to economic status, the richer paying more and the poorer paying less, and limited to those who are expected to benefit from the service resulting. There are conflicting considerations here. It may be very important for a person's self-respect that he contribute equally with his richer neighbour; and unless carefully handled, the identification of a "poor" group which contributes nothing or contributes less, may be humiliating and resented. If levels of contribution are permissive, then each potential contributor can make his own decision. At one extreme there is little justification for the confiscation of a poor widow's hen to help pay for a secondary school that she will never be able to send her children to. On the other hand, if some degree of persuasive pressure is not exerted, there will be those in the community who could contribute but refuse to do so even though they will use the service later. President Nyerere faced this dilemma and after at first opposing compulsion came to the

110

view that indolent members of a community should be made to work and contribute. "From each according to his means, to each according to his need" may be an unattainable ideal, but the first half at least is close enough within range in most East African rural communities to justify a determined attempt to achieve it.

Third, policies for participation should be related to the stage of development reached.[1] Typically different regions within the same country are at different stages. In the first stage, as in Turkana or West Pokot in Kenya, the major tasks are finding and using leaders who will help to get development moving through education, infrastructure, opening up markets and movement into the cash economy; self-help may be impossible and the formation of interest groups premature. In the second stage, as found in much of the Coast Province of Kenya and many of the areas which are marginal for arable agriculture, leaders are still important in decision-making, in setting an example, and in adopting innovations, but increasingly a shift of official extension can be directed towards leaders and groups together. Self-help is active, but follows the tendency for the first projects to benefit all or almost all the community, while later and later projects benefit fewer and fewer. In the third stage, as found in the more highly developed high potential smallholding areas of Kenya such as Nyeri and Kisii, interest groups form themselves spontaneously and the progressive farmers can rely more and more on specialized commercial services. It is at this stage that a special effort is justified, to leap over the leaders and the elite groups who can look after themselves,—the co-operative committee of prosperous farmers, the women's groups (Maendeleo ya Wanawake) of their wives and the wives of civil servants—in order to reach, rouse and help the people who have been left out. This can be done through the reorientation of extension services (see pp. 79—83), through encouraging the expansion of membership of existing groups such as the *mabati* women of Tetu in Kenya, through individual extension contacts, and through concentrating attention on those groups which have wider non-elite memberships. In this stage, community development should be less concerned with conventional self-help projects, which will have shown their usual trend towards serving the better-off members of the community (as for example with dips and secondary schools) and official liaison with which can be handled by technical officers. Community development workers should, rather,

1. For a useful three stage analysis of rural development see Hunter 1970b: 26—28.

be concentrating on welfare extension programmes which have a reasonable chance of adoption and success among the less well off members of the community, such as nutrition, vegetable growing, home economics, health and family planning, In this third stage, community development workers often find themselves overtaken by events and initiatives and left standing; but they can, by redirecting their attention to these less privileged groups, again find a useful role.

Fourth, especially in these highly developed third stage areas, a radical reorientation of staff activities is required. Moris (1972) has shown how central directives can be distorted in the course of application in the field, and their original objectives subverted. To reduce such tendencies carefully devised procedures and careful supervision can help. But if staff are to behave very differently, shifting their attention and services away from local elites to local non-elites, they must themselves be convinced that this is right; and they are unlikely to be convinced that this is right merely through the issue of circulars and orders. The SRDP in Kenya showed the potential of a participatory approach to interdepartmental action. Seminars held over periods ranging from three days to three weeks, in which departmental staff heads came together and together thought through problems with some outside assistance, showed that at both divisional and district levels this sort of open participation could yield ideas, consensus and commitment. As so often, the imagination, intelligence and diligence of field staff proved to be far greater than many imbued with the centrist ideology would have supposed. In any reorientation towards equity programmes, a think-tank open-ended seminar approach is a powerful, perhaps essential, means of securing strong commitment on the part of staff.

Fifth, a major if surprising obstacle is the invisibility of poverty to field staff (see pp. 80—82). This can be tackled through preparatory work for the seminars mentioned above. It was through acting as enumerators in a random sample survey of farmers that the SRDP field staff in Vihiga came to perceive the poorer people. To replicate such a survey on any scale might be difficult; but before attending any seminar, staff could be quickly trained to carry out their own small surveys of one or two areas. Various rules of thumb for selecting respondents could be suggested; but in any case it could be a requirement that at the start of the seminar each participant should describe in detail the circumstances of a number of the poorest people in the area where he worked and put forward his suggestions for how they could be helped.

112

Sixth, as with other aspects of managing rural development, the design, testing and modification of procedures is critical. Oddly, university research in Eastern Africa, with a few notable exceptions including those quoted in this chapter, has neglected the detailed dynamics of local participation. In its earlier stages, the experimental opportunities of the SRDP were not being exploited to explore this vital area; yet such exploration, with experimental testing, is surely a very high priority, especially given the likelihood that equity will be a major preoccupation of the 1970's.

Finally, this concluding section will itself be little better than rhetoric, and far from reality, unless there is a very determined political will to reach the poorer people. Fine phrases in development plans do not feed children; nor does public oratory. In the early 1970's an oversimplified impression is that Tanzania and Botswana have the political will and are building the machinery to implement it; that Kenya has the machinery in the form of an efficient civil service, but not the will; and that Zambia may still be having difficulty in creating both the will and the machinery. These judgements may be harsh. But they are needed to emphasize that the end which is sought, a more equitable rural society, is very difficult to achieve; that trying to achieve it is kicking against the pricks; and that the non-revolutionary course towards it requires sustained effort, a high level of management in the rural areas, and above all a credible and consistent political will.

V. Frontiers for planners

"To plan is to choose"
                              Julius K. Nyerere

"To choose time is to save time"
                              Francis Bacon

1. Perspective

In this chapter some of the frontiers of planning activities for rural development are explored. The word "planner" is used to describe the professional technical staff and the senior field staff of planning ministries, and those who work in planning units in other ministries. Planners are thus mainly but not only economists. The general theme is that planners and their time are scarce resources which require careful allocation. Possible new or expanded activities for planners are discussed. It must be emphasized, particularly for the reader who skips, that it does not follow from this discussion that more planners are necessarily a good thing, nor that it is necessarily desirable that these frontier activities should be undertaken. The argument is, rather, that issues of how many planners there should be, who they should be, where they should be located, and what they should do, deserve to be confronted more explicitly and decided in the light of a wider range of possible activities, costs and benefits than has been usual.

Government planners, like any people who influence major decisions, are easy to criticize, but they are perhaps especially vulnerable in the sphere of rural development. In the past their training, experience, inclinations and work requirements have often biased them to concentrate on the urban, industrial, capital investment, quantified and quantifiable, foreign aid and cash economy aspects of development to the neglect of the rural, agricultural, recurrent expenditure, unquantified and unquantifiable, self-reliant and subsistence economy aspects. Many of them have been trained as economists, have mathematical aptitudes, and need numbers in order to exercise their professional skills. Whether foreigners or nationals, their experience and inclinations have often been mainly urban, with ignorance or rejection of the rural semi-subsistence economy. Their work requirements present them with a heavy load of appraising, processing and negotiating projects, often with a queue of would-be donors and foreign investors. Work pressures and sometimes explicit instructions from a high level confine them largely or entirely to the capital cities where they live and work. It is scarcely surprising to find a disproportionate amount of their time taken up with tasks not directly related to rural development, and that when they are concerned with rural development they concentrate heavily on the cash sector.

But any critic of the work of planners does well first honestly to examine his own motivation. Resentment can easily distort judgement. University staff sometimes suffer from a sense of lack of power and responsibility compared with civil servants. The agonizing choice between being a man of thought and a man of action with which Plato wrestled in the Gorgias lives on today in some of those who have to choose between being university teachers or government servants. Jealousy may be most acute among political scientists and among teachers and students of public administration, since their advice and skills are less likely to be requested or valued by governments than those of economists or even sociologists, and even their research faces special problems. (Nellis 1966.) The tension becomes more acute where many or most of the planners are foreigners, and many or most of the university critics are nationals. It can be valid in its own right to criticize an independent government for being dependent on foreign advisers (although in Kenya and Tanzania in 1973 foreign advisers no longer appeared to play a decisive part in major policy-formulation). But the possibility must be recognized that such criticism subsumes, masks and legitimates expression of the resentment which the man of thought feels for the man of action, and which will persist long after the last foreign advisor has left. If these possible tendencies can be offset, it is easier to take a balanced view of the longer-term issues at stake.

In the longer term it is more relevant to examine what planners do than who they are. The issue of what planners do and what they should do has been fogged by some of the writing about aspects of planning. This appears particularly clearly with econometric model-building which may reflect more the satisfaction of the perfectionist intellectual drives of the authors than the realities of what happens or can be made to happen in planning offices. The classic exchange in

115

East Africa between Clive Gray, representing the practical planner, and Paul Clark, representing the academic analyst, illustrates the two poles of the arguments about what planners do and should do (Clark 1965; Gray 1966; Clark 1967; Gray 1967). As Gray pointed out, plan-writing occupied only a small fraction of the planning office's time once a five-year plan had been published, and, as he says of the Planning Division in Kenya,

by far the major portion of our staff time was devoted to working out pro-cedures for project review and implementation, analysing specific projects in practically all fields, assessing the economic prospects of individual crops and livestock enterprises, advising on the relative allocation of development resources between the former White Highlands and the former African areas—in short, looking at virtually all the operative economic issues facing the government at that time (1964/5)

(1966:2)

Given the importance of these activities, planners' time had a high opportunity cost and would have been misused if extensively applied to econometric model-building or to attempts to use such models pre-dictively. In any case the usefulness of the models, given imperfect and missing data (as described for Nigeria by Stolper [1966]) and the heroic assumptions needed in order to build them, can be seriously questioned. It was not through model-building but through preventing bad projects (of the sort that so easily slipped through during the pre-planning, colonial era), anticipating and planning for future needs and conditions, and advising on major issues in the management of the economy, that planners in the 1960's made some their major and vital contributions to national development. But one of their values was their versatility, so that they might be found engaged on a wide range of tasks from plan-drafting to attending inter-ministerial committees, from dealing with donors, to monitoring project implementation, from financial control to preparing answers to parliamentary questions and even speech-writing. Indeed, a common complaint among planners was how much of their time was taken up with work that did not fall within their own, would-be narrower, definition of planning.

Not surprisingly, rural development has often been a casualty of these pressures. Even where a determined attempt has been made to recruit into planning both national and foreign staff—agricultural economists, rural administrators, and sociologists—with relevant rural experience, they have usually been posted to the centre and then remained there chained to their desks. Sometimes this has been by deliberate instruction from a high level—a prohibition on "wasting time" visiting rural areas. Sometimes it has been by force of circumstance, dealing with an overload of work, much of it generated by other planners. Sometimes arrangements have been made repeatedly to make visits outside the capital, only to be cancelled because of other demands, often from the highest level. At the extreme, as in Lusaka in 1973, the impression could be of so much communication about rural development back and forth between the ministries that there could be but little output to the rural areas. Perhaps there is some analogy with the lemurs of Malagasy which live in isolated colonies held together, it seems, by their mutual need for garrulous quarreling. Where economist planners are of different nationalities, the time and energy taken up with such exchanges may be especially marked, holding them like a magnet in the centre. The Intensive Development Zone programme in Zambia may be an extreme case. Staffed in early 1973 by no less than eleven planners of at least three nationalities, all in Lusaka, it was having great difficulty after years of gestation in achieving any programmes on the ground. More generally, the fact that there were 74 established posts for economists in Lusaka in 1972 and as far as the Working Party reviewing the system of decentralized administration was aware, not a single economist or planning specialist in the provinces (Republic of Zambia 1972:96—7) may be taken as a pathological example of megalocephaly in planning bureaucracy. Perhaps these are warnings too that, unless checked, colonies of planners in capital cities may so generate work for one another and so stimulate the demand for more planners that they take off into self-sustaining growth even if the economy does not.

To blame only the planners for these problems would be unfair. Like field staff and peasant farmers their behaviour can be understood in relation to their experience and work environments and there is no reason to suppose that their responses are any less rational. The explanation for these problems lies partly in the management of planning: the recruitment of foreigners with no local experience and of different nationalities to work on the same project, short spells in posts for nationals and short contracts for expatriates, reliance on the Russian roulette system for posting staff which seems endemic in some of the less efficient agencies of the United Nations, the adoption of oversophisticated techniques which generate shock-waves of demands for sophisticated information that only more planners can provide, and delays in decentralization of staff and discretion to field levels.

Part of the explanation, too, lies in the shifts of perception and priority which take place over time. In the earlier stages of pioneering planning in Eastern Africa it was understandable that there should be some false casts: for example, that econometric model-building should at one time have been a major academic concern. But perceptions and priorities move on, and Colin Leys could write in the late 1960's that ". . . it is difficult not to feel that a radical shift to planning is required —from logical models of plan-making to behavioural models of plan-making: and from models of plan-making to models of planned behaviour" (1969:275). The shift towards rural development has also been gradual, with time lags in experience and recruitment. Moreover, devoting planning resources to rural areas has opportunity costs, and it has only been in the late 1960's and early 1970's in Eastern Africa that staffing positions enabled governments to post planners, whether economists or not, to regions and provinces. Now, however, most countries have field staff with planning competence and intend to have more. This raises more acutely than before the questions:

— what planning activities need to be carried out?

— in particular situations, what ought planners to do?

The answers to these questions must vary by country and region. Some obvious activities for planners who are posted to the field include servicing development committees, administering block grants, liaising between province/region and the centre on development planning matters, and assisting interdepartmental liaison and planning where several departments are involved in the same project or area. In addition planners in the field might sometimes undertake the introduction of improved systems for programming and implementing rural development projects and programmes. But for both field and headquarters planners, there are three other activities which can be examined as frontiers in rural planning, namely evaluation, rural research and development, and area plan formulation. These will be considered in turn.

2. Evaluation

Here and elsewhere in this book a distinction is made between "appraisal" and "evaluation": appraisal is *ex ante* assessment; evaluation is *ex post*, although if it is useful it will also have an *ex ante* character by feeding into future decisions and policies.

Attempts at *ex post* assessment of rural development programmes have a long history which could be traced back through colonial monthly and annual reports; but evaluation as an activity to be mounted systematically with special procedures or personnel is recent. It stems from three main sources.

The first source is North America where a combination of factors combined to make evaluation something of a new industry in the latter 1960's. The introduction into the United States and Canadian governments of PPBS (programme planning and budgeting systems) requiring the specification and measurement of indicators of achievement for public programmes coincided with the development by social scientists of social indicators (see for example Bauer 1966). Another powerful influence was the mounting concern with the design and performance of social action programmes in the United States leading to the involvement of social scientists in monitoring and evaluating their progress and advising on their organization and content (Moynihan 1969; Weiss 1970).

A second source was widespread criticism of international and national aid organizations for the alleged and real shortcomings of aid programmes. This criticism created a need for agencies to defend themselves and also improve their operation. One method adopted was to discuss, encourage and institutionalize evaluation. In view of the public exposure and mixed record of the technical agencies of the United Nations it is perhaps not surprising that one of them should have been in the van (UNITAR 1969). In view of the formidable anti-aid lobbies of the United States and of the pioneering of evaluation in that country, it was also to be expected that USAID would be a leader among donor organizations in appointing mission evaluation officers and in requiring procedures to be followed in systematic programme evaluation (Agency for International Development 1970; Practical Concepts Incorporated 1971).

The third source of the stress on evaluation was less externally derived although externally supported, and more closely related to rural development. As the complexities and difficulties of rural development became increasingly recognized in the 1960's, and as the number and range of social scientists and their research in Eastern Africa dramatically increased, so the linked ideas of research, experiment, evaluation and replication gained currency. The Swedish-supported

119

Chilalo Agricultural Development Unit (CADU) in Ethiopia was a leader in this field; its massive financial and technical assistance input included an in-built evaluation unit. This helped to develop, out of successful experiments in a small area, a programme (known as the minimum package programme, and involving credit, fertilizers, seeds and ploughing equipment) which could be adopted nationally in ecologically suitable areas. In a similar vein in Kenya, the early papers outlining proposals for the SRDP suggested that the programmes should be experimental, should be evaluated, and that replicability outside SRDP areas should be a criterion of success. The experience with SRDP evaluation contains a number of lessons of general value.

With the SRDP it was proposed from an early stage that evaluation should be mounted by the Institute for Development Studies (IDS) in the University of Nairobi. It was under the auspices of the IDS that the survey of 14 divisions in Kenya was carried out in 1968 by university staff in collaboration with government and with the help of graduate students from Princeton (Heyer, Ireri and Moris 1971). In the event the main programme was delayed by the long time it took for the University to prepare its report. In the meantime a build-up of evaluators in IDS overtook the main programme. Following joint government-university seminars, IDS evaluators moved out to live and work in the programme areas, but often before there was anything to show on the ground. In these circumstances, they were certainly not in a position to conduct any *ex post* assessment of projects: they could either work operationally to help the main programme to get going; or they could concentrate on the research which fell within their disciplinary interests. Working operationally laid the evaluation exercise open to criticism within the University for being too close to government, involving work which should be carried out by government, and wasting research resources: and these criticisms were sometimes incongruously influenced by the tide of opposition in American universities to defence contract work for government, as though rural development in Kenya were somehow in the same moral category as the war in Vietnam. But the alternative to working operationally was concentrating on research which fell within evaluators' narrower disciplinary interests, which exposed them in turn to government criticism for being academic and irrelevant. Difficulties were compounded coincidentally by the phasing of the University transition from a predominantly expatriate to a predominantly nationally staffed institution, which was at a stage when the more desirable posts in teaching departments had been Africanized but the IDS, with few permanent established posts, was still mainly staffed by foreigners on short-term contracts. The outcome of these various pressures and tensions was a gradual withdrawal of evaluators from field bases; involvement of researchers increasingly in devising, testing, and evaluating programmes and procedures in collaboration with government staff; and a diffusion of evaluation activity to include more University staff from teaching departments, culminating in an evaluation report on the programme as a whole and on individual projects in particular (IDS 1972). Many problems and opportunities are revealed by the SRDP experience and by experience elsewhere, and various sources are drawn on for the observations which follow.

The purposes and methodology of evaluation can be made to appear impeccable, as they usually are in public and official documents. The purposes are said to be to examine the costs and benefits, performance and effects of action programmes, to tease out the lessons learned, and to present recommendations, based on these findings, to abandon, reduce, expand or modify a project or programme. The words "objective", "independent", and "scientific" are mixed in various proportions, giving an impression of white coats and test-tubes, of clinical impartiality, and of conclusions and recommendations that will be based on the irrefutable authority of scientific research. In practice, however, evaluation faces very serious problems of methodology, of experience and motivation among participants, of organizational and political relationships, and of choices in resource use. All of these were encountered in the SRDP evaluation, but all of them are general experiences. They will be considered in turn.

Some of the more obvious and important problems of methodology are:

— *experimental method:* in rural development, particularly where several different programmes are running concurrently, it is difficult and, if possible at all, extravagant in resources, to mount experiments according to the classical design of studies with random samples, controls, carefully monitored treatments, measurement of effects, and attribution of effects to causes. Certainly in Kenya the ecological, geographical, social, economic and political variations between rural areas are so marked that geographical controls are at best of highly questionable value. Also, a long period may be needed for the identification and observation of "before" and "after" effects, given the slow diffusion associated with much rural change. Moreover, rural development cannot wait for other factors to be held constant while single inputs or single programmes are implemented. Finally, multiple causation poses serious puzzles of interpretation: most of the effects which can be identified as benefits in rural development can be attributed to alternative causes or inputs, or combinations of these. Thus a carefully and professionally designed experiment in the SRDP involved so many treatments—farmer selection, training, credit, access to inputs, and extension follow-up—that it was difficult to determine their relative importances and complementarities in promoting adoptions of hybrid maize. (Ascroft, Röling, Kariuki and Chege 1973.)

— *targets and indicators:* target-setting is an important management tool in improving planning and performance, and evaluation may then be geared to measuring achievement against the target. This form of evaluation is liable to bias activity and effort towards achieving outputs which are quantifiable and measurable to the neglect of those which may be more important but which are less easy to quantify and measure. Care is therefore needed in choosing targets and indicators. Public sector projects in rural development and their outcomes can be seen as long causal chains linked by hypotheses (if a, then b, then c, etc.). Any evaluation system has to select points along the chain at which to carry out examinations and measurements. Various systems can be devised for categorizing stages, two of which can be quoted here by way of illustration:

USAID (1970)   Inputs → Outputs → Purposes → Goals

Dahlgren (1970) Activities → Production targets → Products (outputs) → Sub-goals → Main objectives

In these examples and also more generally, there is a clear distinction between inputs (finance, staff time, equipment, materials) and outputs (loans disbursed, farmers trained, miles of road constructed). Measuring these and assessing their quality can be a valuable activity from which lessons can be learnt about project effectiveness. It may be especially useful to evaluate those outputs which pass from the public to the private sector. But once in the private sector evaluation becomes much more difficult. Causal links may have been postulated between outputs and purposes and between purposes and goals in the USAID system, and between products (outputs) and sub-goals and be-

122

tween sub-goals and main objectives in the Dahlgren system. But multiple causation, hidden processes, exogenous factors, and sheer lack of local knowledge and deficient judgement often make it very difficult indeed to achieve a useful degree of certainty in evaluating the operation of these links. The value of these concepts—purposes and goals, or sub-goals and main objectives—is less in evaluation and more in the planning stage, forcing planners to specify objectives (as persuasively advocated by Heyer 1972) and to state the causal links which they think will operate.

— *unanticipated or unspecified effects:* Rural development programmes usually have multiple effects, only a few of which will be specified in an evaluation plan. Some of these may be anticipated, others unanticipated. Of the unanticipated effects, some may be harmful: for example, malnutrition on an irrigation scheme which substantially raised farmer incomes (Korte 1973); reduced employment for water carriers as a result of a reticulated water scheme (Jakobsen, Ascroft and Padfield 1971:421); or drunkenness when husbands on a settlement scheme monopolized the incomes from pyrethrum to the detriment of their families, provoking their wives to uproot the crop and plant food instead. And some may be beneficial: learning by participants in the development process, and the fostering and growth of managerial capacity are two common examples (Hirschman 1967). Unless an evaluation design is open to changes, and unless perceptive and open-ended research is undertaken concurrently with evaluation, significant unanticipated effects may easily be missed.

— *changing goals:* The goals of programmes are dynamic variables and change over time. The SRDP is an example. It originated in a concern with school-leavers and rural employment; it shifted towards a concern with rural incomes, with an assumption that incomes were connected closely with employment; and then it began to move towards a concern with equity and income distribution. Any rigid evaluation design set up in the early stages would have focussed on school-leavers, in whom there was diminished interest in the early 1970's, and would have paid little direct attention to equity and income distribution. There is, thus, a disadvantage in setting a course in evaluation which it is intended to follow over a long period. In the words of Chairman Mao "There are no straight roads in the world" and while it is sure that the road will twist it is difficult or impossible to be sure in advance where those twists will lead.

— *observers' values:* Evaluators and operational programme personnel may hold values which are additional to or different from those of the programme's rationale, and these personal values may change over time. These values should be taken account of. They should not be masked, or wrapped up in what are really normative statements masquerading as descriptive statements of fact. As Myrdal argues in Asian Drama (1968:32—3) observers' values should be made explicit; and evaluative judgements made against them should be recognized and accepted for what they are. Here again, there are dangers in a rigid framework which might exclude observations of this sort.

The pitfalls and problems of evaluation work are not by any means limited to methodology. There are often serious problems of the experience and motivation of the evaluators. It should be clear from this outline of methodological difficulties that flexibility in approach is necessary. This in turn implies a non-routine, innovative, and sensitive performance by evaluators. But more than this, it requires common sense; a sense of what is practicable, and good judgement if the evaluator is to make the leap from the exposition of facts to the presentation of good recommendations. Some social scientists shrink from that responsibility. Others are so flattered when asked for advice that they go far beyond the bounds of prudence and jump to conclusions not justified by the evidence, sometimes with disastrous results (Moynihan 1969). It is asking a lot of a social scientist, whether he be in a university or in government, to make programme recommendations which require an assessment of the organizational and management aspects of implementation unless he has a training in management or relevant managerial experience. This is perhaps one reason why so many of the proposals which are made are never implemented. One way of improving the chances that recommendations will be implementable is to give priority to discussion and exchanges of ideas between the evaluator who will make the recommendations and the manager who will be faced with implementing them.

Self-discipline can also be a serious problem. Among academics it is common to find a pathological syndrome, the central feature of which is an inability to manage a personal work programme. Subject to the multiple demands of teaching, supervision, examining, research and university politics and administration, they refuse to recognize that the time and energy they have left over from the basic activities which take priority day by day are continually eaten into by unexpected

124

events, and that within that margin a series of time-bounded demands (a paper for the conference next week, a lecture to this group or that course) will continually decimate their capacity for other activities. Most learned in their subjects, they cannot and do not learn from their own experience. In consequence, evaluation reports from universities to governments are invariably (in any experience) delivered late, whatever their excellence in other respects; and it is a commonplace that worse decisions taken on less information but in a more timely fashion are often better than less timely decisions based on more information.

A second problem is the research and status motivation of academics. It is not just a question of publish or perish; it is also a question of conducting work which will be academically respectable. This is liable to bias attention towards narrow special interests which lack the breadth necessary to provide data on which policy decisions can be taken, and towards a style of presentation which is vulnerable to the well-worn criticisms by civil servants of jargon, unintelligibility, inconclusiveness, long-windedness,[1] and unimplementability. The danger is not only that evaluations will be delivered late, but that when delivered they will be either not understood, or if understood, not usable.

Third, evaluation is vulnerable to political insecurity and pressures. External evaluation may be called upon for three reasons, or for combinations of them: to be quasi-judicial; to be supportive; or to improve performance. The quasi-judicial evaluation is expected to apportion credit or blame, usually where a programme has gone seriously wrong, and particular individuals have hopes that it will exculpate them and perhaps place blame on others; the supportive evaluation is called for in order to buttress the organization by showing that it is doing good work, that it is open to evaluation and that it is managerially sophisticated; but most common of all is the evaluation the main purpose of which is to improve performance. All three types and their combinations are expected to affect the future of the organization and of its personnel. Consequently, the evaluator may be regarded as a spy, an investigator, or an enemy; but it is at least as likely that he will be co-opted into the system. Co-opted evaluators resemble parasites in their concern not to kill their hosts; and there is a danger that their reports will be muted in criticism and overlavish in praise in order to secure their continued employment or the chance of another job.

1. Presented with a long draft of a university evaluation report one Kenya Provincial Commissioner exclaimed "You expect me to *read* all *this*? And it is only a *draft!*"

What evaluators do is, and should be, closely related to the fourth aspect, the use of resources. Evaluators are themselves a scarce resource, especially in less developed countries. Where a development programme is in difficulties, the evaluator may be faced with a moral dilemma: whether to become operationally involved; or whether to sit on the sidelines and watch the programme struggle and perhaps founder. It is probably more often right for the evaluator to become involved operationally than he is likely to judge. The experience of programme initiation and management is valuable to him and to his future work in its own right; but more powerfully, where rural development is difficult and a programme may fail for lack of a few pushes or reforms, it is difficult to make a case for keeping clear of involvement. It is hard, for example, to criticize the evaluation officer with the Lushoto Integrated Rural Development Project in Tanzania who spent most of his time organizing the export of vegetables to urban centres; the benefits from this were probably much greater than they would have been from an evaluation study of why the programme failed.

One compromise which was found by some participants in the evaluation of the SRDP was to become involved in the design, introduction, monitoring and evaluation of experimental programmes. The maize credit programme for smaller farmers in Vihiga, the training, credit and extension programme in Tetu, and the management systems described in chapters 2 and 3, were all the outcome of working very closely with government staff and could not have been achieved otherwise. A major lesson of the SRDP is that a great deal of work, sustained over months or years, is required in conducting this sort of operational experiment as opposed to evaluating it from a distance, and this may partly explain why so few university staff have so far seized, or been able to seize, the unusual experimental opportunity presented by the SRDP. The lesson seems to be that for devising and introducing new approaches in rural development it is best to rely mainly on the staff of research institutes or on government planners, providing in both cases that they can be protected, indeed insulated, from the day to day demands of administration, allowing them to concentrate undisturbed and full time on experimental work.

Up to this point, evaluation has been discussed largely as an activity carried out externally, by a university or other organization, not by the government itself. But several governments have set up (albeit sometimes oversophisticated) project evaluation units, and in Eastern Africa, very sensitive programmes of high political priority such as *ujamaa vijijini* in Tanzania and the Intensive Development Zones in Zambia, have discouraged outside research and proposed or mounted their own internal evaluations. Even with these organizations, many of the problems described above are likely to apply, though without some of the disadvantages of a university-based evaluation operation. In any case, much informal and unsystematic evaluation already takes place within governments, through the experience gained with implementation, through personal impressions and through the feedback of internal reporting systems, irrelevant to evaluation though so much of their content may be.

In the SRDP, as it became clear that external evaluation would not, and perhaps should not, provide a continual feedback on performance, and that this was properly a function of the government machine itself, an attempt was made to devise a set of internal evaluation procedures which could be operated by the Area Co-ordinators. (Belshaw and Chambers 1972.) A basic principle was that the conventional rather ritualistic quarterly or annual reports should be avoided, and that reviews should be strictly functional and so timed as to fit into the annual cycle of estimates preparation. Three reviews were proposed each year and implemented in 1972—an Annual Implementation Review, an Annual Evaluation Review, and a Half-Yearly Review.

The Annual Implementation Review was written towards the end of the financial year and, in conjunction with the PIM system (pp. 43—48), made use of the record of experience in the programming charts and monthly reports to present a considered statement on the experience with implementation. It concentrated on the internal operation of the government machine and on public sector outputs, assessing these against targets where appropriate, pinpointing problems and bottlenecks, and making recommendations for the future. Its contents were, for any one area:

- a summary list of projects
- a project by project summary of progress
- a review of project implementation across all projects
- a review of strategy in the light of implementation experience
- a list of projects for programming in the next year.

This last item was related to one major objective of the review, which was to assess experience in time for it to be used in the following

127

financial year's programming exercise. But the review was also sent to officers at different levels in government and thus provided the Area Co-ordinator and the local-level staff for whom he spoke with an opportunity to identify bottlenecks which were outside their control, the resource constraints they experienced, and the policy and procedural changes which would help them in their work. The Half-Yearly review, written after the first six months of the financial year, was largely an interim implementation review, in time to feed into the supplementary estimates for the current financial year and to affect the estimates for the following financial year.

The Annual Evaluation Review was much more difficult, since it was concerned mainly with the impact on the private sector—the people who were the reason for the projects in the first place. The SRDP experience was that a comprehensive evaluation review involved much work and paper, and unless it was very simple, was too difficult and burdensome for Area Co-ordinators to compile on their own. Nevertheless, an appraisal of development effects of selected projects, even if non-quantified and subjective, can be useful, particularly in forcing staff to think about the private sector impact of their work. In the case of the SRDP, the priority attached to evaluation and replicability seemed to justify a serious attempt to develop fairly full evaluation reviews. In other programmes, however, a simpler approach, giving such quantifiable data on impact as may be obtained easily together with subjective assessments will usually be preferable; and external evaluation resources can be used selectively for priority programmes. Ideally, evaluation reviews can be timed so that they feed into plan formulation, which will often mean no more than the annual estimates procedures.

Several lessons and conclusions for government internal evaluation can be culled from SRDP research and experience:

- routine reports in governments often pay little attention to project implementation and negligible attention to evaluation of impact, tending ritually to record statistics of trivial planning value
- a review of implementation experience over a year, tied in with programming, can be an effective way of dramatizing and focussing attention on bottlenecks and problems
- reporting on the impact of projects on the private sector is liable to be burdensome and difficult for staff and should be carried out selectively and often subjectively, perhaps supplemented by external

evaluation resources. The burden of an evaluation review can be reduced by combining it with an implementation review

- any systematic but simple procedure requiring staff to evaluate the projects on which they are working is likely to have benefits in heightening their awareness and in communicating their problems upwards to levels at which some of them can be tackled.

The frontier for planners here is not in the obvious and prestigious activities of setting up complex computerized evaluation systems which may never work, or if they do work, which may demand so much data that they impede implementation; it is in examining the reporting and evaluation systems which already operate within governments and trying to improve them and link them up functionally with remedial action and with future resource allocations. This leads us once again into the realm of procedures and management, which planners have not always been willing or able to explore; but such exploration in the field of evaluation deserves to be considered because of its potential for improving the design and implementation of rural development programmes and projects.

3. Rural research and development

The frequency with which co-ordination of rural research and development work is called for reflects the complexity and variability of the subject matter, the many disciplines involved, the character of researchers, and their physical and institutional dispersal. The variety— physical, ecological, infrastructural, social, economic and political— to be found in the rural areas of any one country is often staggering— ranging from near-desert inhabited by nomads to densely settled irrigation projects, from plains marginal for arable agriculture to high potential mountainous zones, from scattered homesteads to nucleated villages, from precarious subsistence to secure cash-cropping. The disciplines involved include all the social sciences and most of the pure and applied natural sciences including medicine and engineering. The researchers involved, like their colleagues throughout the world, have territorial tendencies, are independent of mind, resent a directing authority, and are partly motivated by a desire for professional recognition and advancement quite largely through publications which lead to acclaim by their peers, preferably on an international level. The researchers are also physically and institutionally dispersed—in government departments, on university campuses, in agricultural research stations, and in the scattered field situations which they choose for their work.

In all these circumstances it is scarcely surprising that communication is often poor. The big advances in the applied natural sciences—new seed varieties like hybrid maize, controls for plant diseases, forms of prophylaxis and treatment for tropical human and animal diseases, better systems of pasture management, more appropriate forms of technology, and so on—come usually from the efforts of co-ordinated teams of researchers and only more rarely from the work of gifted individuals. But the big advances in the social sciences such as understanding the rationality of the small farmer's "conservative" behaviour, unravelling urban-rural linkages, and describing the informal sector of employment and what school-leavers actually do—have usually been the outcome of unco-ordinated individual pieces of research and informal communication between those engaged on them. From a national point of view the priorities, breakthroughs and developments resulting from social science research are liable to appear to be rather haphazard and largely the outcome of researchers' own preferences. For both social sciences and the relevant natural sciences, it seems sensible to ask whether research could be better planned and what part planners might play in this.

Four topics will be examined:

- agricultural research
- the use of local knowledge
- rural R and D and equity
- the organization of research

(i) Agricultural Research

The errors and irrelevancies of much past agricultural research have been part of the received wisdom of rural development in East Africa for at least a decade. They have included inappropriate recommendations deriving from agricultural research stations sited in atypical areas of exceptionally high rainfall (rather like early mission stations which were put on hills and in rainier places) or with peculiar soils; research conducted on pure stands of crops when farmers in practice very

130

sensibly grow mixed stands (in order to spread and reduce risks, to retain moisture, to exploit complementaries in nutrient demand and supply, and to reduce weeding as with maize and beans); fertilizer and spray treatments which for most farmers are inaccessible or uneconomic or both; and accumulated fertility on the soils of research stations resulting from successive fertilizer and manuring trials and leading to unrepresentative conditions and exaggerated yields.

Perhaps more seriously, inappropriate research designs imported from the developed world have very often meant that agricultural research is seeking answers to the wrong questions. The clearest example is trying to increase yields per unit of land rather than yields per unit of labour, although for farmers it is usually labour, not land, which is limiting. In 1972, for example, in an area near the Okovango Swamp in Botswana where land was abundant and where farmers were reluctant to grow cotton, an agricultural research station was persisting in trying to increase yields per acre without even measuring the labour inputs; and this is by no means an isolated example.

Agricultural experiments have also neglected the small farm situation in other ways. At the time of planting the small farmer naturally gives priority to his food crops and plants cash crops only when he has assured his food supply. Necessarily, therefore, his cash crops will be planted later than optimal. Yet research stations have persisted in experiments designed to produce recommendations for cash crops which assume timely planting. Only recently, notably in Nigeria, have experimental programmes begun to be designed around the more realistic assumption of late planting. And this has been achieved only after long argument and sometimes bitter criticism by agricultural scientists.

Agricultural research has also been hobbled by a rigid statistical framework, a straitjacket of respectability, and an excessive reverence for neatness and certainty. Conventional, careful, safe research may sometimes be necessary, particularly where staff changes are likely to mean that experiments have to be handed on to new staff to complete. But the contrast with the benefits which sometimes derive from a more inspired, original, and daring approach can be startling. Two illustrations can be taken from Southern Africa: Gus Nillson in Botswana, a plant pathologist who left official work to set up as a highly successful pioneer of seed-breeding in disease-free conditions; and Allan Savory in Rhodesia who developed a revolutionary system of short duration grazing in which stock numbers are *increased* in order to shift the grazing habitat up the ecological succession. Both these men were professionally qualified and pioneered methods of enormous potential economic importance, and yet both were out of favour with Ministries of Agriculture which had themselves failed to open up these lines of development.

There are many explanations of these weaknesses in government agricultural research. Research stations have been largely or entirely staffed by expatriates who have often been on short-term contracts, who have needed time to begin to understand their local environment, and whose work has been misdirected by the cultural and research design biases they have brought with them from the developed world. Sociologists have until recently been virtually unknown on research stations, although they have become increasingly common on rural development feasibility studies generally. Economists have been rare, yet they have a vital contribution to make to decisions about research priorities and in inducing economic attitudes among biological scientists; for, as Mbilinyi has pointed out (1972:15), most scientific researchers cannot answer the simple question of how much a farmer has to pay to adopt their recommendations. There have also been serious discontinuities of staff and understaffing of institutions. In Botswana at one time there was a period of four years with no officer in charge of pasture research. Serious rundowns in agricultural research capability also occurred in Tanzania in the late 1960's and more recently in Uganda. In contrast, the independent pioneer like Nillson or Savory can usually ensure his own continuity, is not bound by a rigid experimental design, and can often obtain better results than research stations through making quick and sensitive adjustments.

In spite of these difficulties, much good research and development work has been done, for example in the development of hybrid and composite maizes, in Coffee Berry Disease control, and in cotton variety breeding. Many of the weaknesses mentioned have been tackled. Trials of intercropping cotton with food crops have been conducted in Eastern Kenya. Variety breeding increasingly takes account of the probabilities of low fertilizer applications and untimely planting. Economists and sociologists have occasionally been brought in as research staff (for example in Nigeria). The desirability of longer contracts for expatriate research staff is well understood. But very serious problems of perception, knowledge and relevance remain. Agricultural research is still often inbred, inward-looking, encapsulated in the narrow confines of the barbed wire fences and geometrical plots of the research station, and segregated from the practical world of hard work and hard decisions on the small farms nearby. Three ways of breaking this isolation can be suggested. Each illustrates an approach which can be used in other disciplines and other programmes of rural research and development.

The first approach, frequently advocated (Belshaw and Hall 1969; Mosher 1969:6—8) is the use of field trials to bridge the gap between research station findings and the farmer. Such trials are not demonstrations but extensions of research experiments. They have the advantage of preventing overhasty recommendations, of testing innovations in different ecological conditions, and of showing the extension staff what the potential is so that they will have confidence in the advice they pass on to the farmers. Experimental smallholdings as a means of checking out research findings under realistic resource and management levels have also been advocated and introduced on a limited scale in Uganda and Tanzania for testing cash crop systems and also in Uganda to check upon nutritional aspects of alternative farm systems. The principle here of testing innovations in a range of representative conditions should not be limited to agriculture: it applies also to other rural development initiatives.

A second approach is to improve communication between research staff and extension staff. It is a frequent complaint that these two branches of agricultural administration are isolated from one another (Heyer, Ireri and Moris 1971:58—9; ILO 1972:147). Extension staff rarely visit research stations and research stations are usually linked upwards towards the capital city rather than outwards into their local environments. Various measures can reduce these defects. The field trials already mentioned can be conducted jointly by research and extension staff. It can be a routine requirement that agricultural officers visit research stations at regular intervals and that research staff similarly make field visits. Conferences, seminars and workshops can also be held at which information, ideas and requests are exchanged. In other rural research and development work too the principle applies that arrangements are needed to bring together those engaged on research and those concerned with implementing the outcomes of research.

A third approach is to adopt a deliberate and supervised policy of requiring research staff to spend substantial periods exploring the environments in which the results of their experiments are likely to be applied. At one level straightforward geographical exploration is

133

useful. But at another and perhaps more important level, research programmes might become much more relevant and productive if more use was made of the knowledge of local inhabitants. It is a sad reflection on the gap between the social and biological sciences that it should be necessary to make this point. The hard fact is that farmers and pastoralists, despised or ignored though they are by many scientific researchers, are a rich source of information relevant to the choice and design of scientific research programmes.

(ii) The use of local knowledge

In considering the use of local knowledge for research and planning purposes, a first step is to recognize the biases and limitations of scientific data, surveys and categories, and the wealth of accumulated experience and knowledge of local inhabitants. Examples can be taken from rainfall and from vegetation and soils.

Meteorological data often have gaps and are open to suspicion of misreporting from rainfall stations. Also, some rainfall stations are sited in micro-climates of exceptionally high precipitation. An example of the weakness of these data was finding, after ten years of research in East Africa on crop water balance methods of determining potential crop productivities and locations, that the meteorological data available in most areas of Kenya were not adequate to indicate what should be grown where. On the other hand, the farmers living in an area have intimate and detailed knowledge of the weather and of micro-climates, and have their own words for seasons, types of weather, and crop conditions. Their shrewd ideas of what will grow where may be much more accurate and cheaper to obtain than the elaborate outcomes of years of sophisticated research.

Again, surveys of vegetation and soils are very expensive to conduct and are at the same time liable to miss crucial details. In Mbere Division in Kenya, an area marginal for cultivation, micro-environments make a vital contribution to agriculture. These are areas of impeded drainage which flood during rains and on the fringes of which crops can be grown; narrow strips of alluvial soil beside streams where crops flourish; and isolated protected situations suitable for bananas. But individually these are so small that they may not be picked up by a highly professional soil survey of the area. Indeed, economic evaluations of soil surveys, identifying to what extent if at all they are put to use, are long overdue. It might prove far cheaper, quicker and more

134

useful to carry out a more flexible form of ecological mapping in collaboration with the local inhabitants, combining the expertise of scientists with the knowledge of the people. The scientists would have to be patient and might need to learn the art of asking questions and listening to answers. But they could expect to learn much from the categories used by local inhabitants, the ways in which they identify favourable combinations of soils and micro-climates by their use of plant indicators, and their interpretations of the colour, texture and behaviour of the soil. The outcome of such collaboration might well be surveys which are much less expensive and much more usable.

An example of using local knowledge for quasi-scientific purposes is an expedient adopted under pressure during a consultancy on range management in the Northeastern Province of Kenya (Chambers 1969 c). It became clear in the course of investigation that there were strong tensions between predominantly cattle-owning and predominantly camel-owning Somali groups, and that these were related to the different needs of cattle and camels for browse and grazing on different soil-vegetation associations at different times of the year. Any attempt to determine optimal land uses and political spheres of influence had to be based on knowledge of the distribution of these associations, which the Somalis described by names for the soil types. For some parts of the Northeastern Province, geological maps gave soil types, although the categories were not always consistent between contiguous maps, and some of these soil types coincided with Somali categories. The Somali categories also varied but with less sharp discontinuities than those of the geologists. By naming and plotting many water points and fixing their positions approximately by asking elders the walking times between them and other known points, it was possible to cover much of the map with names. Groups of elders were then asked what the soil types were at these places and responded immediately and decisively. Their responses cross-checked closely with the geologists' maps where these existed, and by combining these different forms of data it was possible to draw a soils sketch of the whole area, and then to begin to assess the relative importances of different areas to camel and cattle owners. In addition, long conversations with elders elicited much information about animal husbandry.

This may not seem at all remarkable; the approach is only common sense. But many government servants and scientific researchers are not inclined to spend much time listening and learning. They either think they know already, or somehow fear to ask, or do not know how to, or are insulated from contact with the local inhabitants by their habit of rushing out and back from their offices or homes or headquarters, always in a hurry and never with time to spend a day or two learning. The cost is great. The failure to consult and collaborate with the people who live in and know an area has all too often allowed bad, irrelevant or unnecessary research and led to research results which are difficult or impossible to use.

This is, then, a proper area for intervention by planners if by no one else. The implication is that research staff should be required and prepared to spend days and weeks in the field asking questions and listening to answers. The challenge now is to develop procedures, lists of questions, and even simulation training for this approach. Not only would farmers' problems, behaviour and rationality become clearer to researchers, but researchers themselves would almost certainly change their ideas about the environment they are studying and their own research priorities.

(iii) Rural R and D and Equity

Less obvious but no less important issues for planners' attention concern the relations between research decisions and rural equity. Although this is often not recognized, almost all decisions about research priorities in the rural sector have implications for equity. But these implications are not always obvious.

Decisions about what staff to recruit for agricultural research may seem far removed from questions of rural income distribution. Yet the balance of professional qualifications recruited may determine the extension programmes ten years later. If plant pathologists predominate, plant breeders may shift priorities so that the varieties they develop are less disease-resistant but can be protected by various treatments. If there are few plant pathologists, plant breeders may give a higher priority to breeding for disease-resistance. The outcomes of these alternatives may powerfully affect rural income distribution. In the first case, the new higher-yielding variety may require an expensive protective spray which is beyond the reach of the smaller farmers and which extension staff deliver only to the larger farmers. In the second case the new disease-resistant variety may benefit the better-off farmers less, but may be accessible to many of the poorer farmers.

It is not only the staff who are recruited, but also the criteria which govern policy decisions in the course of agricultural research programmes, that should be monitored and influenced by planners. Agricultural scientists, however professionally competent they may be, are not always aware of the implications of the choices which they make, and a planner with a wider perspective may be able to improve the quality of decisions taken. For example, a plant-breeder may not fully recognize the implications of a choice between developing a stable synthetic and developing an unstable hybrid. But for the poor farmer the difference is profound. The stable synthetic he buys once and then uses the seed year by year without any need for further contact with officialdom or with the market in order to buy seed. The unstable hybrid forces him each year to find cash to purchase new seed. On equity grounds there is indeed a strong case for biasing research and development programmes towards those improved varieties which require fewer and cheaper inputs and which do not require seed renewal. Left on their own, agricultural scientists might, in this context, take the wrong decisions.

Similar considerations can be brought to bear on other research choices: among social scientists whether to study the better-off areas or the worse-off; whether to study the richer or the poorer people in the area; what aspects of their environment and behaviour to study—whether, for example, to pursue traditional social anthropological concerns of kinship and ritual, or questions of social and political relationships bearing on access to resources; among engineers whether to develop tools for tractors or for animal power; among management consultants whether to devise means of providing government services for a wider or narrower section of the society, and especially whether to concentrate on high-level management in capital city, region/province and district, or whether to go down to the point where policies make contact with rural people. The question has to be asked to what extent decisions such as these about research priorities should rest with the individual researcher and to what extent they should be authoritatively determined.

(iv) The Organization of Research

It is always tempting to recommend some central national organization to control and direct research. This is specially so when new concerns arise and research seems slow to fasten on them, as perhaps with the issues of distribution and equity which in many parts of the world are moving into the centre of debate. For government research, central direction with participation by economist-planners is desirable. For natural sciences research generally, particularly where large research resources are involved or where the choice of research is likely to determine future technologies, there is also a case for control and direction. With the social sciences outside government, however, any powerful central authority would have heavy costs. It would be liable to impose yet another bureaucratic obstacle between the research idea and the action, to inhibit the application of research resources and even drive them away, and to annoy researchers. There must also be some doubt about the effectiveness of control, since social science researchers concerned with rural development typically have a high degree of autonomy. Nor is it helpful to ignore their motivation. They do not like being directed or co-ordinated. Moreover, it is a national asset to have a body of lively, active and largely independent social science researchers who pursue what to them seem to be the most important issues. In the field of rural development this freedom enables and speeds changes in perception and policy in government which might otherwise never come about or at best take much longer.

A better system is to organize seminars and to provide forums for discussion of research proposals and research results which can be attended by both academics and planners. The seminars, workshops and conferences organized by the Institute for Development Studies in the University of Nairobi present a good example of how effectively such an approach can work and what useful outcomes can emerge (see for example IDS 1971 and Barnes 1972). Such occasions provide for informal exchanges and contacts between government staff and research staff and in practice lead to mutual influence without the adverse effects of authoritarian direction.

Another useful initiative is to bring together groups of government and university staff to deal with particular subjects. Two examples can be quoted from the Kenya SRDP.

The first example was an area research committee convened for Mbere Division. Membership represented agricultural research, farm management, agricultural extension, agricultural economics, and economic planning, drawn partly from local-level institutions and partly from the centre, and including university as well as government staff. The committee concerned itself initially with classifying ecological zones, identifying crop diversification possibilities, designing crop trials at the field level, and then siting them in relation to the ecological zones. The presence of agricultural economists contributed to an unusual but sensible attention to marketing opportunities and constraints. An extension of this device is implied in the recommendation of the ILO Report for Kenya (1972:147) which recommended the appointment of "a capable and experienced team of agricultural and social scientists" to study semi-arid and medium potential areas. In general, with the qualification that meetings are time-consuming and time has costs, there is a case for considering extensions of this approach, creating groups for each of the major ecological zones in a country.

The second example concerns communication between natural scientists themselves. In connection with area plan formulation in Kenya, a committee was convened to review natural resources data which might be used in agricultural planning. It was only when this committee met that it became clear that, whatever its other benefits, the crop water balance data resulting from ten years of research could not be used to prescribe zones for crops because of the inadequacy of meteorological data. To the social scientist it is alarming to discover the lack of communication between natural scientists within countries and between countries. The intervention of planners to bring scientists and researchers together and to ask them questions about the relevance of their research appears a proper and necessary planning activity.

Finally, as a technique for organizing research and development, there is much to be said for an experimental set of programmes on the lines of the Kenya SRDP. A geographical focus for research brings research workers together without, necessarily, any formal co-ordination. An experimental rationale and the opportunities it presents can encourage them to come to grips with the real issues of what is practicable. The government's need for experimental programmes provides an *entrée* and incentive to university staff. The criterion of replicability acts as a discipline to fix attention on the practical value of what is done. The SRDP presents an effective if low profile example of how rural research can be managed, an example which other countries besides Kenya might benefit from adopting.

4. Area plan formulation

A more conspicuous and conventional frontier for planners has been area plan formulation. "Plan formulation" is used here to refer to the more formal processes of analysis and decision-making which are associated with the allocation of public sector resources or which through incentives or penalties influence private sector resource allocation decisions. "Area plan formulation" relates to this process for a particular geographical or administrative area. Plan formulation has often been considered to require the production of a plan document, but it is by no means limited to this nor does it necessarily require it.

In Eastern Africa in the 1960's and the early 1970's area plan formulation received attention for several reasons: the vogue for "planning" diffused from the capital cities; unfortunate experiences with local authorities encouraged a shift towards decision-making by local-level staff of government departments; and there was an emphasis on local participation and a desire that the national plan should in some way incorporate local wishes. Four approaches can be separated out for the purposes of discussion: the budget process; target disaggregation; shopping lists; and resource use strategies.

First, allocations to rural areas are made continuously on an annual basis through the public sector budget process. This tends to be routine and rarely involves any radical reappraisal or any systematic evaluation of past experience. Typically, local-level staff put in bids based on the previous year's estimates and after some iteration between local level and centre and between ministries in the centre, recurrent and staff allocations are made with a slight increase over the previous year. For all its continuous and rather routine nature, this process has potential for procedural innovation which might improve the quality of the estimates and the projects and programmes proposed in them.

Second, some very crude area plan formulation was attempted in Kenya and Tanzania in the early and mid-1960's through target disaggregation from the national plan down to local levels (Chambers 1973:16—17). The intention was that each province or region and each district would have growth targets which would add up to the national totals. In practice this was largely a paper exercise and it is doubtful whether the targets were ever taken seriously or whether public sector resource allocations were at all closely related to the targets. In the latter 1960's this approach was discredited and abandoned.

Third, and more persistent and important, has been the shopping list approach. Most countries at one time or another have undertaken an exercise of asking regions, provinces, or districts to prepare "plans" which it has recognized would consist of lists of capital projects, in the hope that these could somehow be incorporated in the national plan that was in preparation. But the experience has been uniformly unfortunate. In Botswana, the local council staff who were requested in 1967 to draw up local plans did not at first have the capacity to do so, and when plans were eventually prepared they were too late for incorporation in the national plan. In Kenya and Zambia, shopping lists of projects for their respective second five-year plans were sent up from administrative areas and were regarded with despair by central planners who were unable to read, let alone process and take account of, the daunting piles of paper generated. In Tanzania separate plans for Mwanza, Dodoma and Mbeya produced for the second five-year plan were also shopping lists and contained unrealistic assumptions in relation to national targets and financial availability (Berry *et al.* 1971:25—26). In practice, this bottom-up plan formulation with the intention of incorporating the results in a national plan, has so far been a failure; it has become a competition for resources between areas, often with unrealistic bids put in by local-level staff who have a low expectation that anything will happen, and the central planners who have initiated the operation have not thought through the process of handling the resulting voluminous and inconsistent lists of requests. Mounds of papers mouldering and gathering dust in the back rooms of ministries of planning and disillusioned field staff are the two main relics of this approach.

Discredited though it has been when attempts have been made to integrate it with the production of a national plan, a small capital projects shopping list approach does have some virtue if used carefully at the right stage of administrative development. As seen above (pp. 94—100), the block grant system whereby funds for small projects are allocated by the centre to the discretion of local-level staff has generated enthusiasm among staff and developed their capacity to plan and implement. At any early stage of area plan formulation, staff can be asked to recommend small capital projects which will fill gaps in centrally-determined sectoral programmes in their areas. As a major and sustained approach, however, this has drawbacks: the stock of gaps to be filled may be small; the number of small capital projects which do not require new recurrent expenditure may be rather limited; area development may become unbalanced, with a neglect of recurrent resource management and an overconcentration on new capital projects; in the absence of a development strategy for the area it cannot be known to what extent the projects are overcoming constraints in the achievement of objectives; and executive capacity, particularly in the Ministry of Works and in Water Development, may be more limiting than finance, and the outcome may be not an increase in the provision of new facilities and infrastructure but merely their diversion from those areas for which they had been proposed to other areas determined through a local-level political-cum-administrative allocation process. The conclusion must be that this approach should be used sparingly, that its timing is crucial, and that it should be regarded not as a finished and final procedure but as one step in a series of stages in the development of area management.

The fourth type of area plan formulation can be described as the resource use strategy approach. This approach, much espoused and advocated by perfectionist planners, has a powerful appeal. While the forms it may take vary, it may be designed to include resource inventory and appraisal, determination of objectives and criteria for choice between alternatives, a search for and formulation of alternatives, and then choice between them and strategy design, with various forms of iteration between these. Ideally, of course, it should lead through to the working up of projects, budgets and action programmes and then to implementation. In practice the bitter and repeated experience has been that the process is slow, ponderous, given to premature elephantiasis, and exceedingly difficult to push through to implementation. The most common outcome is a large mimeographed document which presents much data about an area and sometimes some suggestions of development strategy, but no detailed realistic or costed action proposals. Examples are prolific: in Tanzania the Geita, Kilimanjaro and Rungwe District plans (Saylor and Livingstone 1969:8; Berry *et al.* 1971:24 and 41); and in Kenya the first SRDP plan for Tetu, the first study for Kitui, the second phase SRDP plans for Busia, Irianyi, North Nandi, Kiharu, South Imenti and Wundanyi (for general details of these areas see Heyer, Ireri and Moris 1971), and the plan documents prepared by FAO for Migori (described by Rasmusson 1972). An attempt in the SRDP to develop and refine this type of approach through the preparation of a rural planning manual (Belshaw *et al.* 1971) was shelved when it was realized through experience with the SRDP and with the resource use strategy approach elsewhere that the operation of such a manual would be more likely to delay and discredit than to speed and establish the value of area planning.

The common pathology of this approach presents three symptoms. First, it begins with an overcollection of data. The 1968 SRDP survey of fourteen areas (Heyer, Ireri and Moris 1971) is an example. It is far easier to include additional questions in a survey than to eliminate questions; and the more competent, knowledgeable and open-minded the questionnaire designers are, the longer the questionnaires will become and the more difficult to administer, process and use. Indeed, there is sometimes an ironical inverse relation between on the one hand the intelligence, knowledge and perceptiveness of the data collection designer and on the other the chances of the data ever being used. There were undoubted benefits from the 1968 SRDP survey, but they were not exactly those expected. The considerable effort required for data processing diverted manpower resources from the preparation of strategy and action proposals to the mechanics of the analysis and interpretation of data. In this respect the delays in processing and the demands made by it actually delayed the SRDP. The main benefits from the survey, in the shorter-term at least, were the informal learning of those who conducted it and who then contributed directly to the preparation of plans, ahead of the formal analysis and presentation of the survey data. Indeed it was largely the drive on the government side to get on with some plans, however imperfect, which saved the SRDP from the premature data-bound paralysis which has consigned many other studies and plans to an early grave.

A second symptom in the pathology of the resource use strategy approach is the preparation of documents by staff from outside the area, often foreigners. In Tanzania the Geita District Plan was written by a French team together with Devplan personnel, the Kilimanjaro plan by a Devplan team, the Rungwe studies by staff from the Afrika Studiecentrum, Leyden, and the strategy proposals for West Lake (which was however more likely than the others to lead through into implementation) by a group from the Institute for Development Research, Copenhagen. In Kenya the original Tetu plan was prepared by two French planners, the Kitui document by a NORAD team, and the second phase SRDP proposals with the assistance of graduate students from Princeton. That these outside contributions should be needed is scarcely surprising: if carefully managed they can have a catalytic effect on local-level staff (as with the Princeton graduates); they may bring in expertise in resource appraisal which is not available locally; and local-level staff lack the time, involved as they are with ongoing projects, to conduct surveys or assemble data. It is very easy to criticize these outside contributions for being predominantly expatriate and those who took part for leaving soon after writing up. These two factors certainly contributed to the difficulties of pushing studies through to implementation and constitute one reason for a sparing use of this approach. But in the late 1960's and early 1970's in Eastern Africa, given manpower shortages, it would have been very difficult to pursue this approach at all without such inputs.

A third symptom is a low involvement and low commitment of local-level staff. Exceptionally, the planner from outside has acted as a genuine catalyst to participation by local-level staff. More commonly, the isolation of the data collection exercise from field staff hierarchies, the remoteness of data processing, and the time-boundedness of the work schedules of the planners from outside have resulted in the preparation of documents without the direct involvement of local-level staff. A further powerful factor has been the rational low expectation by field staff that anything implementable will result from the exercise, or if it does, that they will be in the same post when implementation occurs. The enthusiasm of the outside advisor and the realism of the local-level civil servant combine to make local commitment difficult to achieve.

Against the background of these difficulties, it is easier to appreciate the achievement of the SRDP in Kenya. The SRDP had the supreme advantage of being promoted by an able managerial entrepreneur who was not a perfectionist. The outcome in the first plans for the first phase areas was often proclaimed as a set of disappointing proposals, of "more of the same", of a "houses and landrovers" programme. The achievement was that anything was implemented at all. Once launched it then became possible gradually, as capability was developed, to improve the quality of what was done. The motto for the SRDP in 1970 might well have been *On s'engage, et puis on verra.*

Although the resource use strategy approach is liable to excessive data collection, inordinate delays in processing, an absence of action proposals, a domination by expatriate advisers, and a low involvement of local-level staff, it is useful in situations where major resource use options exist, and may be particularly important where those options are being preempted. Narok District in Kenya is an example, with major choices for land use between various mixes of large scale arable farming, smallholder settlement, pastoral development, and game and tourism—choices which in the early 1970's were rapidly being pre-empted by land adjudication and a scramble for ranches. Wherever soil erosion is prevalent, as in large areas of Kenya, future resource potential and the options for exploiting it are often rapidly being lost. In river valleys where water is scarce and alternative water use choices exist, as in the Tana basin in Kenya, the case for a resource use strategy approach is also obviously very strong. Where controlled changes in human settlement patterns are envisaged—outmigration and settlement stemming from overpopulation as in West Lake Region in Tanzania, the organization of the population of Dodoma Region in Tanzania into *ujamaa* villages, the settlement schemes in Kenya—the approach is also usually justified. A key to success is that planners exercise stringent self-discipline in amassing only those data which are likely to be used and in regarding the end product of their work as realistic action proposals and their implementation.

The disappointing experiences with these approaches to area plan formulation—conservative budget procedures, meaningless target-dis-aggregation, unusable shopping lists, and unimplemented resource use strategy studies and proposals—has driven us into advocacy of a fifth approach—progressive plan management—which involves a phased and gradual introduction of elements of various plan formulation approaches combined with some of the management systems described earlier in this book. Exceptionally, a full resource use strategy approach is justified. More commonly, the preparation of plans should be built up as part of the budget procedures. This can start with identifying gaps in production infrastructure and attempting to fill them through small capital projects, progressing year by year to more ambitious proposals as local-level confidence and capability builds up. At the stage when a full plan can be drawn up, the headings for one set of plan formulation procedures that may be useful is:

1. Essential data including an inventory of major resources.
2. Assessment of the current state and trends of development in relation to population growth.
3. Identification, formulation and appraisal of production projects and supporting infrastructure.
4. Selection of the production strategy.
5. Determination of priorities for social services.
6. Plan appraisal, approval and final preparation as an action document.
7. Programming and implementation.

The plan should be closely linked with the budget estimating procedures in order to avoid the common gap between plan and estimates and that most frequent failing of plans which Kulp aptly describes as "instant obsolescence" (1971:95).

145

Underlying this gradualist approach is a basic premise that there is an important choice of where to start in rural plan management. Our working hypothesis is that the payoffs are often greater from an unconventional approach which begins, not with plan formulation, but with other parts of the management system and which builds up through incremental grafting and modification of procedures to improve public sector performance in rural areas. Not only is a plan document not necessary for starting; preparing it is an unnecessary distraction and impediment. The sharpening of objectives and implementation of existing projects, the gathering of experience with implementation which can feed back into future proposals, improvements in the budget process and allocations, and the organization of search procedures and rural research and development—these are among the activities which may have higher and earlier payoffs in improved performance. The frontier in area planning is, then, to abstain from premature plan formulation and to explore, develop and evaluate other activities and procedures from which greater benefits may be gained. In short, the frontier lies much less in plan formulation than in the development of management procedures.

5. The management of planners

Up to this point we have only lightly discussed plan formulation in terms of choice; but "to plan is to choose" is of course basic planning philosophy. Planners' paradigms vary in their detail, but commonly include identifying objectives, elaborating alternative ways of achieving those objectives, and then making a rational selection between the alternatives judged against criteria related to costs in scarce resources and benefits in objectives to be achieved. Such a model has seductive intellectual and professional appeal. To criticize it can even appear boorish and unaesthetic. But accepted narrowly and uncritically, it can be dangerous and inconsistent: dangerous because it is liable to preempt planners' time and energies, especially in the elaboration of alternatives; and inconsistent because it is liable to ignore the prior and more critical choice in resource use, namely how planners should allocate their time between alternative activities. For in Eastern Africa in the 1960's and early 1970's planning capability has often been inadequate. To be consistent, planners should manage their scarce selves according to their own paradigm: they should identify their objectives, elaborate alternatives, and make a rational selection of activities. This too has costs in their time; but some higher costs incurred in the time devoted to such appraisals might often lead to higher ultimate benefits through better choices of what planners should do.

Such appraisals are especially important for rural development. The variability and complexity of the components and processes of rural development are an intellectual challenge and a constant temptation which too often lure the curious and energetic into more and more complex categories and detail from which prescription is more and more difficult to extract. The most obvious examples are where linear programming is used for the analysis of small farmer situations or for the construction of regional planning models. The mathematical and cultural bias of computer technology demands burdensome collection and processing of data, preempting much time and effort on the part of research economists and others. Another illustration is the length (not to mention cost) of some books which attempt serious analysis and prescription for rural development planning. The contributions of Collinson (1972) and Kulp (1971) are good and full of insight; but they are, respectively, 445 and 665 pages long, even though both authors might argue that to keep the books as short as they are has required heroic oversimplifications. Linear programming analyses and long books such as these bring undeniable benefits, and they have all helped forward the understanding of rural situations and of rural development. But that is not now the question. The question is one of opportunity costs, of whether such lines of investigation should now be pursued into greater complexity or whether the drive should be towards simplification. It is a question of trying to see how to optimize the returns to the time and energy of those involved, particularly agricultural economists and planners.

For agricultural economists, the point has to be made with brutal force that simple quick-and-dirty activities can have very high returns. For example, Hay and Heyer have suggested that in rural production project appraisal variants of this question should be asked: "How much of what is to be produced by whom and sold to whom at what prices, leaving what level of profit or net income?" (1972:F-48). Or again, in almost any district in Eastern Africa an intelligent and well-informed agricultural economist with a practical bent could in a day or two carry out a simple analysis of farm profitability against constraining resources for the current extension recommendations of the Department of Agriculture. He would need a good sense of farming systems, of seasonal labour profiles, of risks, and of the market. But given these,

147

is it to be doubted that he would often come up with useful recommendations for changes of emphasis or detail in programmes? As it is, we see agricultural economists fighting to feed the computers to which they are enslaved; or preoccupied with sophisticated farm management which leads away from simple operations for the poorer many towards more complex operations for the more prosperous few. A radical change of attitude, especially in Ministries of Agriculture, is needed; but this is not very likely to come about. The damage done by the inappropriate agricultural training of the developed world is probably irreversible. Agriculturalists and agricultural economists have been educated away from being able to see as professional or prestigious those simple operations which are most needed.

Planners, too, sometimes suffer from preferences for overcomplex techniques. Often, though, they are subject to such strong demands for results that they do not have time to stray into the byways of intellectual dilettantism. Their problem is rather that they are victims of the bureaucratic situations in which they are enmeshed. The decisions about where they should live and work and what they should do are often not theirs. It is not they who decide whether they live in the capital city or in a provincial or a regional headquarters. It is not they who decide whether they should be engaged in trying to create and operate a computerized project-monitoring and evaluation system which is more likely to slow up than speed development, or whether they should help to reduce the queue of projects waiting for appraisal. Decisions like these are usually determined politically or administratively at a higher level. What matters is that those decisions should be good. Planners are such an important national resource and their potential contributions to rural development are so great that it is right to devote much care and professional attention to those decisions. To do this is not easy. The senior officials and political leaders who are concerned find themselves under heavy pressure from other demands; and the choices with which they are faced are complex. For there are many competing uses of time to be considered besides those —evaluation, rural research and development, and area plan formulation—which have been examined here. There are always many frontiers; but one of the first is and will remain planning the use of planners themselves, choosing how they should use their time.

VI. Principles and Choices

"I've got a little list —I've got a little list"
W. S. Gilbert, The Mikado

The main thrust of this book is that management procedures are a key point of entry and leverage in securing better performance from government staff in rural development. In the past, procedures have received little attention from those who might have been expected to contribute towards their design, testing and evaluation. They have been neglected by management consultants who are inclined to concentrate on the more prestigious and familiar high-level management in which they are anyway more competent; by central government staff, whether nationals or foreigners—nationals often glad to have escaped from the field and foreigners often ignorant of it; by field staff themselves since they have not been trained in the development of management procedures and are anyway unlikely to be rewarded for innovation; and by academics for whom the safe confines of a discipline are attractive or who lack the time, inclination or access to explore the potential of this largely untouched aspect of rural development. It was only the unusual requirements and opportunities of the Kenya SRDP, with its experimental purpose and its aim of sharpening the machinery of government in rural areas, that drew attention to and encouraged work in this field. It is hoped that the evidence and arguments already presented will have persuaded the reader that this is a realm in rural development which deserves further exploration. To help such exploration this final chapter outlines some of the principles and choices thrown up by the experience so far. That these should come at the end of the book and not at the beginning is in an Anglo-Saxon rather than Gallic tradition; but it has its own logic since the principles are revealed by and can be dissected out of the experience; and if they are accepted, they or some of them may provide starting points for any others who launch out into the same field.

1. Principles, modes of thought

The principles and precepts which emerge from the experience on which this book is based can be described at two levels. The deeper level concerns the modes of thought which underlie statements and prescriptions about management procedures in rural development. Seven principles which are to some extent mutually supporting seem to be particularly important, and are described first. At a second, more operational level, but based on these more general principles, are a number of precepts for procedural design. Both the principles and precepts repeat points which have already been made in the more specific contexts of the earlier chapters, but it seems useful to draw them together and present them in one place. The seven modes of thought are:

(i) Empirical not perfectionist

Rural development is highly complex, is a proper field of study for many disciplines, and is full of variety both within a country and between countries. Rural management is difficult to observe and difficult to manipulate effectively. Complexity and inaccessibility can easily combine to discourage the researcher, consultant or senior government servant from exposure to the real field situation and conversely to encourage him to fall back on more abstract thought. This may be highly dangerous. Abstract thought breeds and nourishes perfectionism. It leads away from reality, from what is feasible, and from the cumulative increments of change which can gradually transform performance. It encourages the design and propagation of ideal models which are not only unattainable but also liable to impair rather than improve performance. The perfectionist planner and the intellectual academic are both susceptible to recommending yet more planning—more detailed and specific statement of objectives, the generation and analysis of more data, and the identification and elaboration of more alternatives to choose between. Planning, like politics, is the art of the possible; and perfectionist planning is liable to have two unfortunate effects: generating an insatiable appetite for planners, who are far from costless; and reducing the chances of anything happening on the ground. Exposure to the reality of rural management through accepting responsibility for procedural innovations is a stringent discipline and may even be felt threatening by planners, and more so by academics. Mistakes are made, as we have made mistakes; but the learning process is valuable and should lead to more practical applications than that sort of bad theory which is derived only from the mind without the embarrassment of contact with the confusion of reality. There is here a basic difference of mental set. The development of management procedures can only proceed well if the empirical and not the perfectionist set prevails.

(ii) Systems thinking

Although it is not paraded in this book, systems thinking is basic to the approach used. This mode of analysis accepts a very wide potential span of relevance, seeks to identify interconnections between phenomena, and presents simplifications of complex relationships in the form of diagrams. The clusters of procedures (figure 1) are a simplification of other diagrams (such as Belshaw and Chambers 1973a, figure 1) which were used at an earlier stage to focus and clarify discussion and analysis; and while it may seem that this is a very simple outcome, it is doubtful whether this stage would have been reached without a preceding journey through more complicated diagrams using systems thinking techniques. One advantage of this method is the ease with which shifts in the span of relevance can be accommodated. Thus in drawing boxes and lines connecting them it is always possible to add more so that additional factors can be taken into account. Given that rural development and rural management are complex both in their nature and in their potential directions and forms of change, this device is a very useful, if not essential, tool. It has the great advantage that at the vital stage of simplification a wide range of relevant factors can be taken into account in grouping phenomena. A further benefit is that by identifying the key entities, operations and linkages and presenting these diagrammatically, choices are more easily seen and listed. In the case of management procedures, figure 1 reveals the choices of where to start as choices between boxes (clusters of procedures) and lines (linkages between the clusters) or combinations of these. Without the preceding analysis and this diagram that resulted, these choices would probably have been less clear. Others who work on rural management procedures can be expected to come out with different and more useful categories than those presented in this book; but they may find it easiest to arrive at them by using a similar method.

(iii) Administrative capacity as a scarce resource

Much of the argument of this book has been that there are or could be ways in which the administrative capacity—the capability for getting things done—of field staff could be substantially increased. It remains true, however, that the administrative capacity for any operation is finite, that it is a scarce resource, and that consequently it should generally be used sparingly, with preference for activities which are administration-sparing rather than administration-intensive, and for those which make brief rather than persisting demands (Chambers 1969b). There is, however, a widespread tendency, especially in the higher reaches of governments, to fail to recognize the choices implied by this principle and to allow the use of administrative capacity to be unthinkingly preempted by programmes and projects. This may be particularly serious now in the uses made of the limited capability to innovate procedures for rural development; for although the returns to using that very scarce capacity may be higher in the rural than in the urban sector, and in recurrent resource management than in capital project management, the choice may be obscured by the urban, capital-city, modern and prestigious bias of preferences and activities which, whatever the official pronouncements, influences the behaviour and decisions of many managers, researchers and consultants. The question may be not to what extent scarce centrally-based innovative capacity will be used to increase scarce administrative capacity in the rural areas, but whether it will be so used at all.

(iv) Optimizing, not maximizing

The words "maximize", or "maximum", or the phrases "as much as possible" or "as many as possible" used in connection with rural development and rural management, usually indicate a non-economist author or speaker. Political scientists and sociologists in particular have fallen into a vogue of advocating maximum co-ordination, maximum local participation, involving all groups and all departments at as many levels as possible. This is loose talk and loose thinking. Economists know very well (unless they have been badly trained, or are bad economists) that in complex situations like those of rural development and rural management, in which several scarce resources are involved, in which there are multiple objectives to be satisfied, and in which multiple outcomes can be anticipated, it is misleading to speak of maximizing any one thing. Maximizing co-ordination or integration would paralyze administration. Maximizing local participation would revolutionize the entire political structure of a country. What is required is a series of informed attempts to optimize a number of resource uses in relation to a number of outcomes, not to maximize any particular ones. And this should always be clear if the multiple objectives of rural development policies and the necessarily wide span of relevance in decision-making are borne in mind.

(v) Optimal ignorance[1]

There is a profound bias in the Western way of thinking, with its most obvious roots in ancient Greece, that knowledge is good. Applied to the planning and the management of rural development this easily promotes and justifies unthinking demands for information—demands which misuse executive capacity and culminate in mounds of unused data. Information has costs. It is far easier and more natural to ask for, to gather, and to accumulate data, than it is to abstain from asking, to reduce communication, and to limit the information acquired. The challenge here is formidable: it is to reorient thinking radically, to ask not—what do I need to know?, or the more common versions—what would it be interesting to know?, what ought I to know in order to be able to defend my conclusions?, what have other people asked? what extra can I ask for in order to make my mark? but rather—how much does the information cost? who is going to process and use it? what benefits will accrue? will the results be available in time? what can be left out? what simplifications can be introduced? what do we *not* need to know? This moves against the tradition of research, against the bias of the educational system, and against the drives of curiosity, but is in harmony with the principles that administrative (in this case information-gathering) capacity is a scarce resource, and that in complex situations activities should be optimal not maximal. It requires experience and imagination to know what is not worth knowing, and self-discipline and courage to abstain from trying to find it out.

(vi) Opportunity- versus problem-orientation

The literature of management and of public administration is frequently concerned with problem-solving and problem-solving capability.

1. This expression is borrowed from Warren Ilchman. See also Ilchman and Uphoff 1971:260—2.

The Ndegwa Commission Report in Kenya (Republic of Kenya 1971a) is a conspicuous example. The paths to development are seen to lead through identifying problems and their causes and then through seeking solutions. It helps here to appreciate that there is an overlap in common usage between the words "problem" and "opportunity". It is possible, as in an example from Thailand (personal communication, C. Doggett), to present the existence of underdeveloped land in an area as a problem when it might more normally have been regarded as an opportunity. Notwithstanding this overlap, however, there are two disadvantages in a problem orientation for rural management. The first is its negative connotations. Problems present themselves; opportunities, however, have to be sought out. The solution of problems is liable to maintain a static situation rather than to promote a developmental one. The attitudes are more those of conservative caretaking government administration than those of an aggressive and enterprising management. The second disadvantage is that problem-solving may lead to misallocation of resources. If a programme goes badly, solving its problems may involve devoting more resources to it and incurring elsewhere costs quite out of proportion to the benefits from the programme in question. The repeated attempts of the Kenya Department of Agriculture to persuade reluctant (and it need hardly be added—rationally reluctant) farmers to plant cotton is a case in point. The less cotton they grow, the greater the problem and the greater the resources devoted to persuading them to grow more—preempting extension workers' time, convincing farmers that the government is misguided, and demoralizing government staff. An opportunity orientation, by contrast, would have directed attention to a search for crops which would have been more rewarding for the farmers and to seeking out new possibilities in extension rather than concentrating effort on what was already not working.

(vii) Sophistication in simplicity

The biases of university education, of intellectual excitement, of desires to extend the boundaries of knowledge, of imagination, of drive and energy—indeed of many of the values which are widely accepted as good—are towards complexity. In designing management procedures, the temptation is to introduce more and more requirements and measures, more and more complicated techniques, and more and more elaborate relationships. But such an approach quickly leads to a drop in output and eventually to paralysis. Simplicity has, of course, to be optimal not maximal. To achieve this, ingenuity and courage are needed to devise and use simplifications—through quick and dirty surveys, through collapsing data, through rules of thumb, through the use of proxy indicators—accepting imperfections and inaccuracies as a price it is worth paying in order to improve outcomes; for it is the outcomes which count in evaluation, not the complexities or apparent perfections of the procedures. Given the strong drives towards increasing complexity, a key principle is to be sophisticated in simplicity.

2. Precepts in procedural design

Besides these general principles some related but more specific and operational injunctions can be culled from the experience reported in this book. These may appear rather obvious and common-sense to the reader, but they are so frequently ignored, and we ourselves have so often neglected or been in danger of neglecting some of them, that they deserve to be restated and re-emphasized.

(i) Introduce joint programming and joint target-setting

The evidence from the literature on Management by Objectives (Humble 1969; Garrett and Walker 1969; Reddin 1971) and from the SRDP experience is strong that benefits in motivation, timing, anticipation of bottlenecks, and project performance in general can derive from joint programming and joint target-setting. In joint programming, all those directly responsible for implementation should be present and should freely and willingly contribute their ideas and knowledge. In joint target-setting the subordinate should with his supervisor freely take part in drawing up a work programme and agreeing the targets to be achieved. That these two procedures should be innovations is a sad reflection on the underdevelopment of management in the field administrations in Eastern Africa. They require a different style of management to that of the colonial heritage of a quasi-military hierarchy in which decisions are taken at the higher levels and then passed down for execution by junior staff who are required to obey orders and not to reason why. But not only do they require a new style; they help to generate it. The very procedures of joint programming and joint target-setting bring together staff whose relationships would otherwise be more distant and more hierarchical, and legitimates and requires a freer form of communication and participation in a common task. In the design of any procedures for rural management a high priority should be to identify opportunities to exploit the potential of these techniques.

(ii) Make meetings few and functional

Meetings have costs: they use up staff time and energy. At their worst they lead to frustration and disillusion among the more active attenders, and to a false consensus for poor decisions born of boredom and exhaustion rather than convinced agreement. Meetings should be used sparingly and should be functional. In designing procedures, where meetings are thought to be desirable, the purpose and procedures of the meeting itself should be thought out and specified, together with the expected outcomes and an indication of their usefulness. The costs of meetings in staff time can be reduced by the simple device of starting with those items which are the only concerns of a few people, who can then be released as soon as they have been dealt with. The intervals between meetings can be made longer, as occurred with what were originally monthly management meetings in the SRDP. Or meetings can sometimes be abandoned and a system of *ad hoc* communications or sub-meetings substituted. Meetings can be very important, as they are in joint programming and joint target-setting; and it will be noted that for the meetings described in chapters 2 and 3 the procedures are clearly laid down and the outputs are functional—directly affecting work to be done.

(iii) Make reports short and functional

Most government reporting in rural areas is ritualistic and contains much information that is never used or which, if used, is misleading. Application of the principle of optimal ignorance will usually lead to the elimination of items and to shorter reports. Conversely, identification of functions which can best be fulfilled through reports may show new information of a different sort which should be included. The Monthly Management Report in the SRDP is an example of an attempt to design a strictly functional report, which consequently departed from the normal format and normal distribution of reports. Where routine statistical data are required, they should be recorded on standard forms with a clear and simple layout. The costs of any reporting system in terms of staff time and effort should be weighed against the benefits in information *actually used* and any motivational and learning benefits which there may be for the persons reporting.

(iv) Subsume or abolish old procedures

New procedures are almost invariably additive: a new item is to be reported, a new return to be sent, a new ledger to be kept, a new committee to be set up; but rarely indeed is the new procedure accompanied by the formal abandonment of the old. Occasionally there is a major convulsion and reports are streamlined, returns and ledgers rationalized, and committees merged or disbanded; but these are the exception not the rule. In introducing new procedures experimentally, it may be necessary at first to add the new system while allowing the old one to continue. But such a situation should not be allowed to persist. Where possible, the new system should subsume the old from the beginning. But whether this will be possible will depend on the degree of access and authority of the person or persons who are introducing the new procedures.

(v) Start with a pilot experimental approach

New procedures are usually introduced all at once and then never systematically evaluated. But like any other development initiative, a new procedure should be subject to pilot testing. As with pilot projects generally, there are dangers to be guarded against, including observer effects, unrepresentative conclusions resulting from particular personalities, and other factors peculiar to the experimental situation. A sensible sequence may often be research — design — pilot testing — evaluation — modification — retesting — evaluation and so on, culminating in abandonment or replication. In evaluating new procedures very special care should be taken to allow for unusual behaviour by participants resulting from the experimental situation, particularly if they adopt a deferential attitude towards the researchers. Almost any pilot project can be made to "succeed" in some sense and researchers must be ready radically to modify or abandon what may work in the experimental situation but which is likely to fail with widespread replication. The experience with the SRDP systems reported in Chapters

2 and 3 was that many modifications were necessary in the light of experience, both in the design of forms and in the content of procedures. And it may be noted that at the time of writing, neither of the systems has been replicated.

When replication takes place, a training input may be needed and for this the staff who already know how to operate a management system may be invaluable as trainers. Where a major management system is involved, evaluation should continue after replication. Modifications in different areas or subsequent training inputs may prove necessary.

In order to provide an opening for an R and D input it is not essential to have a full SRDP-type approach. A ministry can decide to designate an area for R and D work without there having to be a national programme like the SRDP. But if programmes involve several ministries then a high-level national (or in the cases of Tanzania and Zambia perhaps regional) decision may be required.

(vi) Involve participating staff in discussing procedures

Participating staff know what they are really doing and this may be quite different from what the designer of the procedures intends or thinks. The literature of organization theory is full of examples of work restriction, of distorted preceptions, of connivance at low performance, of presentation upwards within a hierarchy of information which misleads its recipients. These problems cannot be avoided entirely. But in working out procedures they may be reduced by seeking full and free discussion with those who will use them. The final introduction of the procedures may have to be authoritative; but discussions with participating staff at the design stage and a readiness to modify procedures during testing, are more likely to lead to improvements than to losses.

We must end on a note of caution. In spite of the emphasis which should be placed on procedures, they cannot be a comprehensive panacea. Introduced in isolation, new procedures may be ineffective or harmful, lapsing into bureaucratic ritual or producing unintended results (Molander 1972). Careful monitoring and supplementary management training are minimal safeguards against these dangers. Another pitfall is excessive administrative innovation leading to signs of a saturation psychosis, described by Laframboise for the Canadian civil service (1971). Procedures may be a key point of entry in attempting to improve performance in rural management; but they are not a complete and sufficient answer to all problems nor a means of exploiting all opportunities. In the short term they may even distract attention from those more conventional concerns—training, terms of service, postings and promotion policies, staff development planning, staff evaluation, work travel facilities, housing, the education of the children of staff—which are properly and understandably the concern of management specialists and of field staff themselves. But in the medium term, good procedures will often highlight and provide supporting evidence for the need for reforms in these areas. What we are arguing is that whereas changes in these aspects may require long campaigns waged mainly in capital cities, improved management procedures can be introduced in rural areas more quickly and with an earlier payoff in results.

3. Choices

If governments are as serious about the priority of rural development as the quotations at the beginning of Chapter 1 imply, and if the arguments and evidence presented in this book are generally accepted, then the design and testing of new management systems and procedures for overattention paid to urban as against rural development, to plan should be a component of any policy which seeks to achieve a more balanced use of manpower resources. This applies in rectifying the overattention paid to urban as against rural development, to plan formulation as against programming and implementation, to capital projects as against recurrent expenditure, and to management training for the centre control headquarters as against the field periphery.

More important, however, the success or failure of new rural management systems and procedures may be central to the question of the extent to which rural equity can be approached through piecemeal social engineering as opposed to utopian and revolutionary solutions. A major issue for the 1970's is whether the behaviour of government field staff can be bent away from those who are already better off and directed much more towards those who are worse off. In this, political will is crucial and can by no means be taken for granted. Without it, isolated innovations and scattered well-meaning attempts by a few civil servants will lead to little. But with it, and with a gathering of experience and skills in this field, it may prove possible to reach many more of those who are being left out and left behind and to help them catch up and benefit more from the changes which are taking place around them. At the very least, determined attempts in these directions seem well worth while.

If this first decision—to give priority to developing management procedures for rural development—is taken, then other choices and decisions follow. The first choice is who should undertake the work and where they should be located. Research and development can be carried out by consultants based in a consultancy organization; by staff from central ministries; by field staff; by the staff of central management units such as the Directorate of Personnel Management in the President's Office in Kenya; by research and teaching staff in institutes of public administration; by university teaching staff from departments of management or of government; or by the staff of research institutes.

There are arguments for and against all of these. Let us consider them in turn. Management consultants may have much relevant expertise but of a rather culture-bound type, and may find it uncongenial (just as governments would find it expensive) if they have to spend a long time in rural areas. Government staff in ministries may have field experience and a good understanding of aspects of the current system, but may take a "top-down" view of rural management, and may not be available for long enough periods for adequate work. Field staff themselves do quietly innovate in a limited way, but often without a wide awareness of the implications and without relevant training. Staff in central government management units may be best placed for this work if they can be prised away from their desks and from the flow of tenacious demands which prevent them working in rural areas. Staff in institutes of public administration also appear well located for this R and D work, with the added benefit of gaining experience of what actually happens in rural management and the opportunity of using this in their training courses. University teaching staff are another possibility, but they, like central ministry staff, are subject to strong demands on their time, in their case from teaching, examining and the like. Staff working from research institutes, as we were, may be as well placed as any, particularly if they have a high degree of autonomy in the allocation of their time and lack other pressing commitments. The best policy in any particular country, in the short term at least, is probably to encourage simultaneous initiatives based on a number of different institutions, while keeping communication open between them.

A second choice is what sort of person, with what skills and experience, should be recruited to work on rural management. It goes without saying that wherever possible such people should be nationals whose professional future can be seen to lie in this and related fields. Deryke Belshaw and I were privileged in the experience we were able to gain through the work we did, and parts of this book are an attempt to make that experience available to others; but obviously it is better if those who gain the experience remain as an asset to the country concerned.

In the short term there may be a case for some foreign contributions, for example if seminars or training programmes are required, skills in systems analysis, organization and methods, and various aspects of management may be most readily available from outside. But there are dangers here (see also M. Chege 1973): of the hard sell of the latest trend in management methods; of the culture-bound urban-industrial consultant whose dark suit has never encountered rural mud; of transfers of inappropriate management technology designed for, to paraphrase Nyerere, reaching the moon rather than the village. The most pervasive danger is probably the introduction of excessive paperwork. The mistakes we made should be a warning.

The aim should be to build up a cadre of nationals with experience and expertise in the R and D aspects of rural management. For this the insights of sociology, of organization theory, of management experience, and of agricultural economics appear particularly relevant. We ourselves came to this field from agricultural economics and public administration and found the combination of outlooks useful. But more important than educational and professional backgrounds is a sympathetic understanding of the situation of field staff, a capacity to innovate, and a willingness to work in rural areas. Essential above all is that indefinable sense of what is, and what is not, practicable; and this implies that those with administrative experience may have an advantage over those who have not.

A third complex of choices is where to start. The six clusters of procedures:

- programming, implementation, operational control
- field staff management
- local participation procedures
- evaluation
- rural research and development
- plan formulation,

and the linkages between them (see figure 1) make the choices clearer. Our own conclusion is that there will often be higher and quicker benefits from starting with programming, implementation and operational control than with the other clusters, and that the process of developing and diffusing management procedures should be seen as a sequence over time, starting simply with the PIM system or something like it and gradually moving into greater complexity as and when it seems desirable. One possibility is to start with an annual programming exercise and then gradually move over the years into action plan formulation tied in with budget procedures.

The choice of where to start will depend, however, on a number of local factors, not least who is available to make the start. If, for example, a capability exists in a department of community development in conjunction with a provincial or regional administration, local participation may appear an appropriate entry. If a ministry of agriculture has adequate central staff, rural research and development may be a relatively easy entry point. The clusters do not, indeed, necessarily have to be linked. There is no overriding reason why initiatives should be connected. Nor is there any reason to regard procedures as a specially difficult field which should not be touched without a mastery of the magic of modern management and systems analysis. Let nothing written here inhibit anyone from trying to improve whatever practices are current. This is a field which no discipline has claimed and which lies open to all. It is one in which common sense, imagination, sensitivity and patience are more important than any formal qualifications. There are many civil servants who are in a position to start at once and exactly where they are, with the practices they use to manage and communicate with their staff and which it is within their discretion to vary. They can begin piecemeal, and without delay. The main thing is to start.

4. Concluding

Managing rural development is not a new activity. It is going on all the time. What is perhaps new is treating management procedures for rural development as a field for systematic research and development and suggesting that it should be a concern not only of civil servants but also of others, including university staff. For too long students of public administration have been failing to contribute to national development, to their own frustration and that of their mentors, because of the preoccupations of the development administration movement (for a critique of which see Schaffer 1969) and because of the wide gap between researchers and the actual detailed, mundane but vital processes and procedures by which government bureaucracies operate. I hope that this book will help to show that this futility need not persist; that there is an opportunity for useful work; that those whose field of study is public administration can, as has already been done in Kenya (Chabala *et al*. 1973), examine procedures, comment upon them and their effects, and suggest modifications. The only valid excuse for public administration academics who complain that their work is not useful to governments should be that they lack access. Lack of professional competence is scarcely an excuse in an activity which is as uncharted as this. Competence is gained by doing, by plunging in and gathering experience on the run while bringing to bear those wider perspectives of which university staff should pre-eminently be aware. There emerges a strong argument, therefore, for departments of government or public administration in universities shifting focus to include research and development in rural management procedures. This would, as again already in Kenya, have the added advantage of gradually creating a national resource of former students with experience, skills and insight in this field.

Taking a wider view, what matters is that more people, whether civil servants, university staff, students or others, should be concerned with procedures for rural management, that more new approaches should be tried, and above all that the findings should be written up and become part of the stock of public and international knowledge. There are powerful reasons for the exchanges of knowledge and insight being direct between the countries where rural development is a priority. But first that knowledge and insight must be made explicit. There is already a wealth of experience locked up in the minds and memories of civil servants but which they have hitherto rarely analyzed or presented. Procedures have tended to be regarded by them as well as by researchers as a rather dull part of the job, not worth much attention, and certainly not worth writing about. If this book has begun to show that to the contrary they are an exciting field for innovation, that they are worth writing about, that there is value in sharing experience, it will have served much of its purpose.

If rural management becomes a major concern, then the evidence and arguments presented here will be seen as preliminary, partial and fumbling. No doubt some of the conclusions will turn out to be premature; no doubt some of the generalizations will prove to be wrong. But the purpose has been to try to open up the subject and present possible starting points for others. As with research and development work generally, it is not easy to forecast with any accuracy the potential of this field of activity. It may be great. What we need, and need quickly, is a clearer appreciation of the extent of that potential. This will only be possible if others launch out into this challenging and exciting area. If they do not, a major chance may be missed. It they do, perhaps they will discover much more effective techniques which can be used for making life better for those, particularly those who are worse off, who live and will continue to live in the rural areas of the third world.

References

Agency for International Development 1970 *Evaluation Handbook*, Office of Program Evaluation, Agency for International Development, Washington D.C., November

Almy, S.W. and P.M. Mbithi 1972 "Local Involvement in the Special Rural Development Programme", in IDS 1972

Anderson, John 1971 "Self Help and Independency: the Political Implications of a Continuing Tradition in African Education in Kenya", *African Affairs*, Vol. 70, No. 278, January

Apthorpe, Raymond 1972 *Rural Co-operatives and Planned Change in Africa: an Analytical Overview*, Rural Institutions and Planned Change Volume 5, United Nations Research Institute for Social Development, Geneva

Ascroft, Joseph, Carolyn Barnes and Ronald Garst 1971 "The Kisii SRDP Survey of Farm Level Enterprises: a Preliminary Report of Findings", Working Paper No. 5, Institute for Development Studies, University of Nairobi, November

Ascroft, Joseph, Niels Röling, Joseph Kariuki and Fred Chege 1973, *Extension and the Forgotten Farmer: First Report of a Field Experiment*, Bulletin Nr. 37, Afdelingen voor Sociale Wetenschappen aan de Landbouwhogeschool, Wageningen

Barnes, Carolyn, ed. 1972 "Harnessing Research for Production, Dissemination and Utilization", Occasional Paper No. 5, Institute for Development Studies, University of Nairobi

Bauer, Raymond A. ed, 1966 *Social Indicators*, MIT Press, Cambridge, Mass.

Belshaw, D.G.R. 1968 "Agricultural Extension, Education and Research", in G.K. Helleiner, ed. *Agricultural Planning in East Africa*, East African Publishing House, Nairobi, pp. 57—78

Belshaw, D.G.R. and Malcolm Hall 1969 "Economic and technical co-ordination in agricultural development: the case for operational research", *East African Journal of Rural Development*, Vol. 2, No. 1, pp. 9—25

Belshaw, Deryke and Nilam Bedi, Robert Chambers and Jess Hungate 1971 "Rural Planning Manual" (mimeo) (various drafts) Institute for Development Studies, University of Nairobi

Belshaw, Deryke and Robert Chambers 1971 "Programming, Operational Control and Evaluation for Rural Development Plans", Staff Paper No.

111, Institute for Development Studies, University of Nairobi

Belshaw, D.G.R., T.J. Bjorlo and M.M. Shah 1972 "A Hierarchical Systems Formulation of the Rural Development Process in Developing Countries", mimeo, University of Nairobi

Belshaw, Deryke and Robert Chambers 1972 "A Functional Review Sequence for Rural Development Programmes: A Procedure for Recurrent Resource Management", Working Paper No. 24, Institute for Development Studies. University of Nairobi, February

Belshaw, Deryke and Robert Chambers 1973a "A Management Systems Approach to Rural Development", Discussion Paper No. 161, Institute for Development Studies, University of Nairobi, January

Belshaw, Deryke and Robert Chambers 1973b "PIM: A Practical Management System for Implementing Rural Development Programmes and Projects", Discussion Paper No. 162, Institute for Development Studies, University of Nairobi, January

Berry L. et al. 1971 "Some Aspects of Regional Planning in Tanzania", Research Paper No. 14, Bureau of Resource Assessment and Land Use Planning, University College, Dar es Salaam

Blau, Peter M. and W. Richard Scott 1963 Formal Organizations: a Comparative Approach, Routledge and Kegan Paul, London

Boesen, Jannik, Anthony Moody and Birgit Storgaard 1972 "Development Problems and a Proposed Strategy for Development Planning in West Lake Region (Bukoba, Karagwe and Ngara Districts)", mimeo, Institute for Development Research, Copenhagen and Bureau of Research Assessment and Land Use Planning, University of Dar es Salaam, December

Brokensha, David and John R. Nellis 1971, in IDS 1971

Bunting, A.H. ed. 1970 Change in Agriculture, Duckworth, London

Butcher, D.A.P. 1971 An Operational Manual for Resettlement: a systematic approach to the resettlement problem created by man-made lakes, with special relevance for West Africa. FAO, Rome

Chabala,H.A., David H. Kiiru, Solomon W. Mukuna and David K. Leonard 1973 "An Evaluation of the Programming and Implementation Management (PIM) System", Working Paper No. 89, Institute for Development Studies, University of Nairobi, March

Chadwick, George 1971 A Systems View of Planning: Towards a Theory of the Urban and Regional Planning Process, Pergamon Press, Oxford

Chambers, Robert 1966 "Harnessing Social Science", East Africa Journal, Vol 3, No. 8, November

Chambers, Robert 1969a Settlement Schemes in Tropical Africa, a study of organizations and development, Routledge and Kegan Paul, London

Chambers, Robert 1969b "Executive Capacity as a Scarce Resource", International Development Review, Vol. 11, No. 2, June

Chambers, Robert 1969c "Report on Social and Administrative Aspects of Range Management Development in the Northeastern Province of

Kenya", Ministry of Agriculture, Nairobi, October

Chambers, Robert and David Feldman 1973 *Report on Rural Development*, Ministry of Finance and Development Planning, Gaborone, Government Printer, Gaborone

Chambers, Robert 1973 "Planning for Rural Areas in East Africa: Experience and Prescriptions", in Leonard, ed., *Rural Administration in Kenya*, pp. 14—38

Chambers, Robert and Jon R. Moris, eds. 1973 *Mwea: an Irrigated Rice Settlement in Central Kenya*, Weltforum-Verlag, Afrika-Studien Nr. 83, Munich

Chege, F.E. 1971 "Packaging and Marketing of Agricultural Inputs to Small-scale Farmers: a research proposal", Working Paper No. 7, Institute for Development Studies, University of Nairobi, November

Chege, F.E. and N. Röling 1972 "The Effect of the Diffusion of New Agricultural and Related Technologies on Income Distribution among Rural People in Kenya", Working Paper No. 65, Institute for Development Studies, University of Nairobi, October

Chege, Michael 1973 "Systems Management and the Plan Implementation Process in Kenya", Discussion Paper No. 179, Institute for Development Studies, University of Nairobi

Clark, Paul G. 1965 *Development Planning in East Africa*, East African Publishing House, Nairobi

Clark, Paul G. 1967 "Development Planning in East Africa: A Rejoinder", *The East African Economic Review*, Vol. 3 (New Series), No. 1, June

Cliffe, Lionel *et al.* 1968 "An Interim Report on the Evaluation of Agricultural Extension", Rural Development Research Committee, Rural Development Paper No. 5, University College, Dar es Salaam, September

Cliffe, Lionel and John S. Saul 1972 "The District Development Front in Tanzania", *The African Review*, Vol. 2, No. 1, June

Cliffe, Lionel and John S. Saul, eds. 1972 *Socialism in Tanzania, An Interdisciplinary Reader, Vol. 1 Politics*, East African Publishing House, Dar es Salaam

Cliffe, Lionel and John S. Saul, eds. 1973 *Socialism in Tanzania, An Interdisciplinary Reader, Vol. 2 Policies*, East African Publishing House, Dar es Salaam

Collins, Paul 1970 "The Working of the Regional Development Fund: a problem in decentralization in rural Tanzania", paper to the University of East Africa Social Science Conference, Dar es Salaam

Collinson, M.P. 1972 *Farm Management in Peasant Agriculture: A Handbook for Rural Development Planning in Africa*, Praeger, New York

Dahlgren, Göran 1970 "An Approach to Systematic Evaluation", Working Paper for OECD Seminar on the Evaluation of the Effectiveness of AID, October 28—30

Dryden, Stanley 1967 "Local Government in Tanzania: Part II", *Journal*

167

—Some Aspects", *Journal of Local Administration Overseas*, Vol. 4, No. 3

Edward, Cecilia G. 1969 "Understanding the Role of Community Development Officer in Embu District, Kenya", University College, Dar es Salaam, Department of Political Science Third Year Dissertation, March

Ellman, A.O. 1967 "Kitete, a Land Settlement Scheme in Northern Tanzania", *Land Settlement and Co-operatives*, No. 1, FAO, Rome

Ferguson, C.G. 1965 "The Story of Development in Malaya (now Malaysia) —Some Aspects", *Journal of Local Administration Overseas*, Vol. 4, No. 3

Gaitskell, Arthur 1959 *Gezira, a Story of Development in the Sudan*, Faber and Faber, London

Garrett, John and S.D. Walker 1969 *Management by Objectives in the Civil Service*, CAS Occasional Paper No. 10, HMSO, London

Georgulas, N. 1967 "Settlement Patterns and Rural Development in Tanganyika", *Ekistics*, Vol. 24, No. 141, August pp. 180—192

Gerhart, John D. 1971 "Rural Development in Kenya", *Rural Africana*, No. 13, Winter 1971

Gertzel, Cherry 1970 "The Provincial Administration and Development in Kenya, 1965—68", Paper to the Universities of East Africa Social Science Conference

Gitelson, S.A. 1971 "The Mubuku Irrigation Scheme: a Case Study", *East Africa Journal*, Vol. 8, No. 5, May

Godfrey, E.M. and G.C.M. Mutiso 1973 "The Political Economy of Self-Help: Kenya's Harambee Institutes of Technology", Working Paper No. 107, Institute for Development Studies, University of Nairobi, June

Gray, C.S. 1966 "Development Planning in East Africa: A Review Article" *The East African Economic Review*, Vol. 2 (New Series), No. 2, December

Gray, C.S. 1967 "Development Planning in East Africa: A Reply", *The East African Economic Review*, Vol. 3 (New Series), No. 1, June

Harrison, R.K. 1969 "Work and Motivation: A Study of Village level Agricultural Extension Workers in the Western State of Nigeria", mimeo, Nigerian Institute of Social and Economic Research, Ibadan, 1969

Hay, F.G. and J. Heyer 1972 "The Vihiga Maize Credit Package", in IDS 1972

Hesse, C. 1968 "Some Political Aspects of Development Planning Implementation in Zambia with particular reference to the Eastern and Laupula Province", Paper to the University of East Africa Social Science Conference, January

Heyer, Judith, Dunstan Ireri and Jon Moris 1971 *Rural Development in Kenya*, East African Publishing House, Nairobi

Heyer, Judith 1972 "Choice in the rural planning process", *East Africa Journal*, Vol. 9, No. 3, March

Hirschman, Albert O. 1967 *Development Projects Observed*, The Brookings

Institution, Washington D.C.

Holmquist, Frank 1970 "Implementing Rural Development Projects", in Hydén, Jackson and Okumu eds. 1970

Humble, John W. 1969 *Improving Business Results*, McGraw-Hill, New York

Hunter, Guy 1969 *Modernizing Peasant Societies*, Oxford University Press, London

Hunter, Guy 1970a *The Administration of Agricultural Development: Lessons from India*, Oxford University Press, London, New York, Bombay

Hunter, Guy 1970b "Agricultural Change and Social Development", in Bunting, ed. *Change in Agriculture*

Hursh, Gerald D., Niels R. Röling, and Graham B. Kerr 1968 *Innovation in Eastern Nigeria: Success and Failure of Agricultural Programs in 71 Villages of Eastern Nigeria*, Diffusion of Innovations Research Report 8, Department of Communication, Michigan State University, East Lansing, Michigan, September

Hutton, Caroline 1970 "Nyakashaka Farm Settlement, Uganda", in Bunting ed. 1970

Hutton, Caroline 1973 *Reluctant Farmers*, East African Publishing House, Nairobi

Hydén, Göran, Robert Jackson and John Okumu 1970 *Development Administration: The Kenyan Experience*, Oxford University Press, Nairobi

IDS 1971 "Strategies for Improving Rural Welfare", Occasional Paper No. 4, Institute for Development Studies, University of Nairobi

IDS 1972 "An Overall Evaluation of the Special Rural Development Programme 1972" (IDS Evaluation Team Report for the Ministry of Finance and Planning), Institute for Development Studies, University of Nairobi

Ilchman, Warren and Norman Uphoff 1971, *The Political Economy of Change*, University of California Press, Los Angeles

ILO, 1972 *Employment, Incomes and Equality: a strategy for increasing productive employment in Kenya*, International Labour Office, Geneva

Jakobsen, B., J. Ascroft and H. Padfield 1971 "The Case for Rural Water in Kenya", in IDS 1971

Joy, Leonard 1969 "Problems of Agricultural Administration and Extension Services", *East African Journal of Rural Development*, Vol. 2., No. 1, 1969

Kang'ela, B.B.C. 1971 "The Problems of the Planning Process in the South Kwale Special Rural Development Programme", Third Year Dissertation, Department of Government, University of Nairobi

Kidd, David W. 1968 *Factors Affecting Farmers' Response to Extension in Western Nigeria*, CSNRD (Consortium for the Study of Nigerian Rural Development) 30, 204 Agricultural Hall, Michigan State University, East Lansing, December 1968

Kidd, David W. 1971 "A Systems Approach to Analysis of the Agricultural

Extension Service of Western Nigeria", Ph.D. thesis, Department of Extension Education, University of Wisconsin, Madison

Kirunda, Charles R.A. 1971 "Problems of Implementing the Rural Development Programme in Ankole District, Uganda, during the 1969/70 Financial Year", mimeo, Department of Political Science and Public Administration, Makerere University, Kampala

Korte, Rolf 1973 "Health and Nutrition", in Chambers and Moris eds.

Kulp, Earl M. 1970 *Rural Development Planning: Systems Analysis and Working Method*, Praeger, New York

Laframboise, H.L. 1971 "Administrative reform in the federal public service: signs of a saturation psychosis", *Canadian Public Administration*, Vol. 14, No. 3, pp. 303—325

Landell-Mills, P.M. 1966 "On the Economic Appraisal of Agricultural Development Projects: the Tanzania Village Settlement Schemes", *Agricultural Economics Bulletin for Africa*, No. 8, December

Leonard, David K. 1970a "Some Hypotheses Concerning the Organization of Communication in Agricultural Extension: a Report on a Small Survey Done in Vihiga Division, Kakamega District", Staff Paper No. 72, Institute for Development Studies, University College, Nairobi, June

Leonard, David K., with Bernhard Chahilu and Jack Tumwa, 1970b, "Some Hypotheses Concerning the Impact of Kenya Government Agricultural Extension on Small Farmers", Staff Paper No. 71, Institute for Development Studies, University College, Nairobi, July

Leonard, David K. 1970c "Some Hypotheses Concerning the Organization of Communication in Agricultural Extension: a Report on a Small Survey Done in Vihiga Division, Kakamega District", mimeo, paper to the 1970 Universities of East Africa Social Science Conference, Dar es Salaam, December 27th—31st

Leonard, David K., Humphries W'Opindi, Edwin A. Luchemo and Jack T. Tumwa, 1971 "The Work Performance of Junior Agricultural Extension Staff in Western Province: Basic Tables", Discussion Paper No. 109, Institute for Development Studies, University of Nairobi, June

Leonard, David K. 1972a "The Social Structure of the Agricultural Extension Services in the Western Province of Kenya", Discussion Paper No. 126, Institute for Development Studies, University of Nairobi, January

Leonard, David K. 1972b "Organizational Structures for Productivity in Kenyan Agricultural Extension", Working Paper No. 20, Institute for Development Studies, University of Nairobi, February

Leonard, David K., ed. 1973 *Rural Administration in Kenya*, East African Literature Bureau, Nairobi

Leys, Colin ed. 1969 *Politics and Change in Developing Countries: Studies in the Theory and Practice of Development*, Cambridge University Press

Leys, Colin 1969 "The Analysis of Planning", in Leys, ed. 1969

Lord, R.F. 1963 *Economic Aspects of Mechanized Farming at Nachingwea in the Southern Province of Tanganyika,* HMSO, London

Maina, J.W. and J.D. MacArthur 1970 "Land Settlement in Kenya", in Bunting, ed. 1970

Makoni, Z.C.I. 1969 "Trends in Rural Development—The Regional Development Fund", University College, Dar es Salaam, Department of Political Science Third Year Dissertation, March

Mbilinyi, S.M. 1972 "Agricultural Research Problems in East Africa", ERB Paper 72.4., Economic Research Bureau, University of Dar es Salaam, September

Mbithi, P.M. 1972 "Harambee Self-Help: The Kenya Approach", *The African Review,* Vol. 2, No. 1, June

Mbithi, Philip M. 1973 "Agricultural Extension as an Intervention Strategy: an Analysis of Extension Approaches in Kenya", in Leonard, ed. 1973

McNamara, Robert S. 1972 "Address to the Board of Governors", International Bank for Reconstruction and Development, Washington, September 25

Mercer, A.M. 1970 "Ol Kalou Salient Project, Kenya", in Bunting, ed., 1970

Millikan, Max F. 1967 "Comments on methods of reporting and evaluating progress under plan implementation", in *Planning and Plan Implementation,* Department of Economic and Social Affairs, United Nations, New York

Molander, C.F. 1972 "Management by Objectives in Perspective", *Journal of Management Studies,* Vol. 9, No. 1, February, pp. 74—81

Moock, Peter R. 1971 "The Vihiga SRDP Farm-level Survey: a Preliminary Report of Findings", Discussion Paper No. 111, Institute for Development Studies, University of Nairobi, June

Moris, Jon R. 1972 "Administrative Authority and the Problem of Effective Agricultural Administration in East Africa", *The African Review,* Vol. 2, No. 1. June

Moris, Jon and Robert Chambers 1973 "Mwea in Perspective", in Chambers and Moris eds. 1973

Mosher A.T. 1967 "Administrative Experimentation as a 'Way of Life' for Development Projects", *International Development Review,* June

Mosher, A.T. 1969 *Creating a Progressive Rural Structure to Serve a Modern Agriculture,* Agricultural Development Council, New York

Moynihan, Daniel P. 1969 *Maximum Feasible Misunderstanding: Community Action in the War on Poverty,* The Free Press, New York and Collier—MacMillan, London

Myrdal, Gunnar 1968 *Asian Drama, An Inquiry into the Poverty of Nations,* Penguin Books, Harmondsworth

Nekby, Bengt 1971 *CADU: an Ethiopian Experiment in Developing Peasant Farming,* Prisma Publishers, Stockholm

Nellis J.R. 1966 "Research and Technical Assistance: a Case Study of Problems for the Political Scientist", Paper to Conference of the East

African Institute of Social Research, Makerere College, January

Nellis, John R. 1967 "The Planning of Public Support for Tanzanian Rural Development", *Journal of Developing Areas*, Vol. 1, July, pp. 477—488

Nellis, John 1972a "The administration of rural development in Kenya", *East Africa Journal*, Vol 9, No. 3, March

Nellis, J.R. 1972b "Report on the Special Rural Development Programme: Calendar Year 1971", mimeo, Institute for Development Studies, University of Nairobi

Nellis, John R. 1972c "Prelude to Arusha: a study of Productivity Problems on a Rural Development Scheme in Tanzania", *Journal of Administration Overseas*. Vol. 11, No. 3, July, pp. 169—181

Ness, Gayl D. 1967 *Bureaucracy and Rural Development in Malaysia*, University of California Press, Berkeley and Los Angeles

Newiger, Nikolaus 1968 "Village Settlement Schemes. The problem of co-operative farming", In: Ruthenberg, Hans (ed.) 1968

Nyangira, Nicholas 1970 "Chiefs' Barazas as Agents of Administrative and Political Penetration", Staff Paper No. 80, Institute for Development Studies, University of Nairobi, July

Nyerere, Julius K. 1968 "Socialism and Rural Development", in Julius K. Nyerere, *Freedom and Socialism: Uhuru na Ujamaa, a selection from the writings and speeches 1965—1967*, Oxford University Press, Dar es Salaam

Nyerere, Julius K. 1972 "Decentralization", Speech to the National Executive Committee of TANU, May

Okai, Matthew (n.d.) "The Adequacy of the Technical Base for the Agricultural Extension Service in Uganda: a Case Study in Lango District", RDR 6, Makerere University College, Kampala

Othieno, T.M., & Belshaw, D.G.R. 1965 "Technical innovations in two systems of African peasant agriculture in Bukedi district, Uganda", *East African Institute of Social Research Conference papers*

Oyugi, W. Ouma 1973 "Participation in Development Planning at the Local Level", Discussion Paper No. 163, Institute for Development Studies, University of Nairobi, February; also in Leonard ed. 1973

Plato *Gorgias* (translated with an introduction by Walter Hamilton), Penguin Books, 1960

Practical Concepts Incorporated 1971 *Some Practical Concepts to Assist Project Evaluation*, Practical Concepts Incorporated, 1825 K Street NW, Washington D.C.

Proctor, J.H. ed. 1971 *Building Ujamaa Villages in Tanzania*, University of Dar es Salaam Department of Political Science, Studies in Political Science No. 2, Tanzania Publishing House, Dar es Salaam

Rainford, R.G. 1971 "Provincial Development Committees in Zambia", *Journal of Administration Overseas*, Vol. 10, No. 3, July

Rasmusson, Rasmus 1972 *Kenyan Rural Development and Aid*, Develop-

172

ment Studies 2/72, Swedish International Development Authority, Information Division, Klarabergsgatan 60, Stockholm

Reddin, W.J. 1971 *Effective MBO*, Management Publications Limited, London

Reining, Conrad C. 1959 "The History of Policy in the Zande Scheme" *Proceedings of the Minnesota Academy of Science*, Vol. 27

Reining, Conrad C. 1966 *The Zande Scheme, an Anthropological Case Study of Economic Development in Africa*, Northwestern University Press, Evanston, Illinois

Republic of Botswana 1968 *National development plan 1968—73*, Gaberones 154 pages

Republic of Kenya 1969 *Development Plan 1970—74*, Government Printer, Nairobi

Republic of Kenya 1971a *Report of the Commission of Enquiry (Public Service Structure and Remuneration Commission)* 1970—71, (The Ndegwa Commission Report), Government Printer, Nairobi

Republic of Kenya 1971b *The Appropriation Accounts and Other Accounts and the Accounts of the Funds for the year 1969/70*, Government Printer, Nairobi

Republic of Kenya 1972a *1972/73 Estimates of Recurrent Expenditure of the Government of Kenya for the year ending 30th June 1975*, Government Printer, Nairobi

Republic of Kenya 1972b *Development Estimates for the Year 1972/73*, Government Printer, Nairobi

Republic of Zambia 1966 *First National Development Plan, 1966—1970*, Government Printer, Lusaka

Republic of Zambia 1971 *Second National Development Plan, January 1972—December 1976*, Ministry of Development Planning and National Guidance, Lusaka, December

Republic of Zambia 1972 *Report of the Working Party Appointed to Review the System of Decentralized Administration* (The Simmance Report), Cabinet Office, Lusaka, printed by Government Printer, Lusaka

Republic of Zambia 1973 *Estimates of Revenue and Expenditure for the Year 1st January 1973 to 31st December 1973*, Government Printer, Lusaka

Röling N. and F. Chege 1972 "A Tetu Extension Management Project: Proposal for an SRDP Experiment", mimeo, Institute for Development Studies, University of Nairobi, November

Ruthenberg, Hans ed. 1968 *Smallholder Farming and Smallholder Development in Tanzania—Ten Case Studies*, Weltforum-Verlag, Afrika-Studien Nr. 24, Munich

Rweyemamu, Anthony H. 1966 "Managing Planned Development: Tanzania's Experience", *Journal of Modern African Studies*, Vol. 4, pp. 1—16

Saul, John S. 1973 "Marketing Co-operatives in a Developing Country. The

Tanzanian Case", in Cliffe and Saul, eds. 1973

Saylor, R. G. 1970 "An Opinion Survey of Bwana Shambas in Tanzania", ERB Paper 70.15, Economic Research Bureau, University of Dar es Salaam

Schaffer, B.B. 1969 "The Deadlock in Development Administration", in Leys, ed., 1969

Shaw, D.J. 1967 "Resettlement from the Nile in Sudan", *Middle East Journal*, Vol. 21 (August), pp. 463—487

Sheffield, James J. ed. 1967 *Education, Employment and Rural Development*, East African Publishing House, Nairobi

Stolper, Wolfgang F. 1966 *Planning Without Facts: Lessons in Resource Allocation from Nigeria's Development*, Harvard University Press, Cambridge, Mass.

Temu, Peter 1973 "The ujamaa experiment", *Ceres*, Vol. 6, No. 4, July—August, pp. 71—75

Thomas, Gary 1967 "The Transformation Approach at a Tanzania Village Settlement", mimeo, Markerere Institute of Social Research Conference Papers No. 427, January

Tordoff, William 1968a "Provincial and District Government in Zambia, Part 1", *Journal of Administration Overseas*, Vol. 7, No, 3, July

Tordoff, William 1968b "Provincial and District Government in Zambia —Part II" *Journal of Administration Overseas*, Vol. 7, No. 4, October

UN 1967 *Local Participation in Development Planning: a preliminary study of the relationship of community development to national planning*, Department of Economic and Social Affairs, United Nations, New York

UN 1971 *Integrated Approach to Rural Development in Africa*, United Nations, New York, Social Welfare Services in Africa, No. 8, July

UNITAR 1969 *Criteria and Methods of Evaluation: Problems and Approaches*, UNITAR Series No. 1, United Nations Institute for Training and Research, New York

United Republic of Tanzania 1969 *Tanzania Second Five-Year Plan for Economic and Social Development 1st July 1969—30th June 1974*, Vol. I, Government printer, Dar es Salaam

Vail, David J. 1970 "Report on the Evaluation of Four of the Initial Sixteen Extension Saturation Projects in Uganda" mimeo, Makerere Institute of Social Research, March

Van Velsen, H.U.E. Thoden 1973 "Staff, Kulaks and Peasants: A Study of a Political Field", in Cliffe and Saul eds. 1973

Waterston, Albert 1969 "An Operational Approach to Development Planning", *International Development Review*, Vol. 1, No. 3

Watts, E.R. 1968 "Forty Years of Crop Introduction: A Study of Agricultural Development in Embu District, Kenya", RDR No. 72, Makerere University, November

Watts, E.R. 1969 "Staffing Aspects of the Extension Saturation Projects in

Uganda", RDR No. 90, Makerere University, Kampala, November

Watts, E.R. 1970a "Agricultural Extension in Embu District of Kenya", *East African Journal of Rural Development*, Vol. 2, No. 1, 1970

Watts, E.R. 1970b "Extension Saturation Project Report. B. Staff Evaluation", mimeo, Department of Rural Economy, Makerere University College, March

Watts, E.R. 1970c "Measures to Increase Extension Effectiveness", mimeo, Paper to 1970 Universities of East Africa Social Science Conference, Dar es Salaam, December 27—31

Watts, E.R. 1971 "Extension Staff Organization in Uganda", mimeo, Paper to the Conference on Comparative Administration in East Africa, Arusha, Tanzania, September

Weiss, Carol H. 1970 "The Politicization of Evaluation Research", *The Journal of Social Issues*, Vol. 26, No. 4, Autumn

Welch, Calvin 1969 M.A. Thesis, Makerere University College, Kampala

Widstrand, Carl Gösta ed. 1970 *Co-operatives and Rural Development in East Africa*, The Scandinavian Institute of African Studies, Uppsala

Widstrand, Carl Gösta ed. 1972 *African Co-operatives and Efficiency*, The Scandinavian Institute of African Studies, Uppsala

Wood, Alan 1950 *The Groundnut Affair*, The Bodley Head, London

Worsley, Peter, ed. 1971 *Two Blades of Grass: Rural Co-operatives in Agricultural Modernization*, Manchester University Press.

Appendix A

Instructions for the Annual Programming Exercise (APE)

These instructions are for the Area Co-ordinator.

Before the APE meeting

1. *Decide which projects should be programmed.* Almost any project can be programmed using this system. Some examples are crop extension, community development training, water schemes, credit, vegetable marketing, road construction, livestock marketing infrastructure, mobile health teams, a health centre, holding grounds, crop demonstrations, rural industries, and so on. The system can also be used for groups of projects designed for simultaneous implementation.

The decision which projects to programme should be taken normally in consultation with departmental officers, unless some other procedure has been laid down. In general, those projects should be preferred which:

- have larger finance and staff requirements;
- involve interdepartmental collaboration;
- have high priority either nationally or locally;
- would benefit most from programming.

Care should be taken to limit the number of projects for programming in order to avoid overloading the Monthly Management Meeting and the Monthly Management Report.

2. *Arrange the APE meetings.* A complex project may take a whole day to programme, while it may be possible to complete four or five simple projects in a day. Programming will become quicker as staff become familiar with the system.

Arrange a timetable.

Book a quiet room where the meeting will not be disturbed and with plenty of room for participants to sit comfortably round a table from which they can see the blackboard. A large blackboard with coloured chalks and eraser is recommended.

Invite those staff who are responsible for implementing the project. This means those who are operationally responsible at the field level and who will be responsible for achieving the targets set. It should also include the officer, often from a higher level, who is responsible for fund releases.

Ensure a supply of Annual Phasing Forms (APFs) (see appendix D) and Annual Programming Charts (APCs) (see appendix E) and any maps or papers which may be necessary.

3. *Brief the Participants.* Where the system is new to all or some of the participants, explain its purpose and operation to them before the meeting. Explain that it is intended to assist staff and to improve implementation. Explain that in joint programming they will be taking part in deciding the timing and targets for the implementation of which they are responsible, and that they will be able to discuss the resources they will need. Explain briefly the APF and APC.

4. *Prepare the Room.* If a blackboard is being used, set it up so that all can see it. It is best, however, if the participants sit equally round a table. Prepare the blackboard to look like an APC except for the parallel railway lines. (See appendix E). Disconnect any telephone.

At the meeting

Conduct the meeting largely by asking questions. Do not try to dictate to the departmental officers concerned. Elicit information from participants. Your function is to help them to produce a realistic implementation programme. You should respect their professional opinions but, through the questions you ask, you can and should raise issues important for implementation.

1. *Ask questions about the objectives of the project.* Sometimes these will not be clear. Who will benefit? Is the project consistent with national objectives? If the objectives prove unacceptable in discussion, or if the approved objectives will not be achieved by the project, or if it emerges that some other project would achieve them better, arrange for further discussions and adjourn the meeting. If the objectives are accepted and the project is agreed as suitable for achieving them, programming can begin.

2. *List the operations required for the project.* Either on the left hand side of the blackboard or on APFs, or on both, list the operations

177

from the top downwards. Each participant must take part and know what is going on, preferably through what is shown on the blackboard, but failing that through keeping his own APF as a working sheet. Encourage participants to contribute ideas about what needs to be done. A checklist can be used but it is valuable for participants to think the project through for themselves. Add and delete operations as necessary. A general checklist of operations is:

Securing approval
Release of funds
Obtaining land
Staff recruitment
Staff training
Housing
Equipment and supplies
Local participation
Operations of implementation (e.g., farm visits, loans issued, etc.)
Evaluation

This is not comprehensive and common sense will suggest others. Many projects do not include all these operations.

3. *List the officers responsible for implementing each operation.* Ask participants to name who is responsible for the implementation of each of the operations, and enter their initials next to the operations on the blackboard (or on the APF). (All those named should be present at the meeting.)

4. *Ask what resources are required for each operation.* Finance, land, equipment and supplies are the most common. Include staff time if this is likely to be a constraint. Note these against the operations and quantify whenever possible.

5. *Agree the timing and targets for each operation.* If using a blackboard, the months of the year should have been marked across the board. Ask what deadlines there are (e.g., crop planting seasons) and enter them against the relevant operations. Ask how much time lead operations such as fund releases will take and mark these in. Then by questioning and discussion enter in bars to represent the expected and feasible periods for each operation. Encourage very free discussion since full commitment only follows from full and free participation. It may be necessary frequently to rub out and alter timing estimates. Ask what indicates completion of operations, and enter these completion indicators, quantified whenever possible, at the right hand end

178

of the board. Enter quantified monthly targets for achievement where possible, asking participants to set their own targets.

The discussion which takes place at this very important stage will often throw up unanticipated problems. Sometimes it will be necessary to adjourn, but usually programming can be completed in one session. It cannot be emphasized too strongly that those taking part must freely contribute and must really think through and feel responsible for their parts of the project.

6. *Check feasibility and agreement.* Allow time for all concerned to consider carefully, following your questions:

- whether any important operations have been left out;
- whether there will be conflicts over staff time use or other resource use between this project and others;
- whether the different operations are correctly timed in relation to one another;
- whether timings and targets are feasible, and whether those responsible for implementation are convinced of this and committed to them;
- what is most likely to go wrong, and what can be done to prevent it.

7. *Transfer to APFs and/or APCs as appropriate* (see appendices D and E).

To complete an APC:

- transfer the list of operations from the blackboard or APF to the APC, putting one operation in each box on the left hand side of the chart.
- Number the operations.
- For each operation fill in the upper "railway lines" in black for the period the operation is planned to take. Mark the start and finish of the period with a short vertical line. (In cases of uncertainty or where an operation is very intermittent, use a dotted line).
- Where there are quantifiable monthly targets, write in the relevant figures above the black line at the end of the months concerned and also above the completion date.
- Enter the completion indicator (the event which shows the operation to be complete), quantified where possible, in the end box.

Each participant should then leave the meeting with a completed record of what has been agreed.

After the meeting

Ensure that those most closely concerned have APFs and/or APCs. If any key person was not at the meeting, follow up personally with a very full briefing. Make sure that you have a full record (as you may have been writing on the board rather than recording on an APF or APC). Send copies to the SRDP headquarters in the Ministry of Finance and Planning. The distribution of APFs and APCs is a matter for your discretion.

Place the APCs for all projects on the wall of your office and keep them up to date so that they provide a quick visual indication of the state of implementation of the projects.

Appendix B

Instructions for the Monthly Management Meeting (MMM)

The procedures for MMMs will vary according to circumstances. They should take account of the purpose of the meeting which is very practical—to report on progress and problems and to plan and agree action for the next month—concentrating on *who* should do *what, how and by when.* The basis of the meeting is the programming which has already taken place in the APE. Suggested procedures are:

Preparation: Before the meeting fill in the first two columns of the first section of the monthly report (appendix F).

Find out the status of those operations (e.g., release of funds, supply of equipment) which are being carried out centrally and which participants may not know about.

Alert your secretary or clerk to be ready to type the Monthly Management Report (MMR) soon after the meeting.

Time: The last week of the month. Avoid departmental pay-days.

Place: A board or committee room is best, to ensure an absence of interruptions. Ideally the APCs should be displayed so that they are visible to all at the meeting.

Attendance: All those who are responsible for implementation should be present. While a very large meeting should be avoided, it may sometimes be desirable for staff to attend from more than one hierarchical level. Care should be taken that the attendance is such that the character of the meeting can be practical and concerned with the hard details of action.

Procedure: The Chairman should be chosen with a view to making the meeting as effective as possible. He may be the senior administrator in the area, or yourself, or the senior technical officer, or members of the meeting in rotation. You may be more effective as executive officer of the meeting than as chairman.

An agenda may not be needed. The projects are discussed in order. The sequence can be prearranged so that those staff involved in only a few projects can be dealt with first and then leave the meeting.

Decide the dates of the next two meetings.

Project by project take the APC and by inspection see what operations should have been completed, or should be active or about to start. Ask the officer responsible the current position. Discussion on action required follows almost automatically. Record the situation and action required for the MMR. Mark in the lower railway lines on the APC in green or red:

green: when an operation is on or ahead of time/target; when an operation should have started and has not but is still expected to be completed on time.

red: when an operation is behind time or below target; when it is not expected that an operation will be completed on time or achieve its target.

When there is a quantified target, record the actual achievement in figures above the lower railway lines on the APC.

Before leaving discussion of any project, ensure that adequate action (by *whom*, *how*, by *when*) has been agreed and that you have the information you need for the MMR.

Other business can be discussed after all projects have been covered, but make sure that the meeting has first dealt with the hard detail of actual implementation. Two common other business items are:

(a) *Project Preparation:* The working up of new projects which have not yet been programmed.

(b) *Reprogramming:* If (i) there has been three months of red and (ii) the original programming has become impossible to achieve, reprogramming can be considered. Reprogramming must not be a device just to avoid red if red is still justified. The reprogramming line (being an extension of the original black line) should be blue or purple instead of black. Reprogramming one operation may lead to reprogramming others. It may sometimes be necessary to start again with a new chart.

Appendix C

Instructions for the Monthly Management Report (MMT)

For specimen parts of a report see Appendix F.

The report is a management tool for securing action from whoever is responsible. It is not at all like a conventional report about rainfall and visits by VIPs. It should be kept short and to the point and not include more information than is needed to guide those whose action is required.

The sequence of the report is:

Monthly Management Report for (Area) for (Month and Year)

Date and place where meeting was held

Those present

Date for next meeting

and then

1. Progress and action summary

This is the most important part of the report. There are six columns in this section:

Project operation: Write in the project underlined. Underneath, list the operations which are or should be active. Prefix operations with their serial numbers from the APCs.

Target by end of month: Very briefly write in what was meant to have been achieved. Use terms like:

in hand = proceeding satisfactorily

in post = appointed and ready to start work

on site = delivered and ready for use

AIE recd = AIE received

Where there is a quantified target, give it.

Actual at end of month: Here write in what has been done, again very briefly. Where there is a quantified target, express the achievement as a fraction.

On time: This is short for "on time or on target". Enter YES or NO.

183

YES is equivalent to green on the APC; NO is equivalent to red.

Action: What needs to be done. Use words like

expedite

order

NFA (no further action)

see 4 c, 5 a (referring to other operations which are responsible for a delay)

By: The initials of who should act. This must be a recipient of the report. Underline the initials when an operation is behind time or target. Circle initials in red on the copy sent to the person who should act.

2. Progress and problems

Use this section to describe and explain in more detail, as necessary, what has happened, project by project. In the right hand margin again place the initials of those who are to act, underlining where a programme is behind time or target. You can also use this section to state the implications of delays.

3. Project preparation

Describe briefly progress and problems in preparing new projects. State action required and use the right hand margin to enter the initials of those who should take it.

4. Any other matters

These may include your work programme, staff movements, visits, and other general information, but should be kept very short.

5. Distribution

The distribution list can be kept on the same stencils and used from month to month. The report should go to:

all who attended the meeting

all those from whom action is requested (at whatever level in government or parastatals).

The initials of recipients should be circled in red on their copies to draw their attention at once to the action required. The report should be in the post or delivered as soon as possible after the meeting.

Appendix D

Specimen Annual Phasing Form

Financial Year 1971/72. Planning Area: Kaguru.

Project: DIPS (11 DIPS).

(1) Operation	(2) Officer(s) resp. for operation	(3) Resources required	(4) Start date	(5) Completion date	(6) Completion indicator (quantify whenever possible)
1. *Secure approval for programme*					
a) By MOA	MOA AC	MOA	1.9.71	15.9.71	Letter received by PDA
b) Proposal to MFP	MOA	MOA	16.9.71	30.9.71	Copy received by PDA/AC
c) Approval by MFP	MFP	MFP	1.10.71	31.10.71	Letter received by MOA
2. *Release of funds*					
a) To PDA	MOA	£ 3,300	1.11.71	14.11.71	AIE received by PDA (£ 3,300)
b) To DO	AC/PDA	£ 3,300	15.11.71	21.11.71	AIE received by DO
3. *Obtain materials*	DO		21.11.71	4.12.71	Material on site
4. *C. D. 1 day programme*	ACDO	C. D. Staff	1.9.71	30.9.72	11 programmes satisfactorily completed
5. *Organize self-help*					
a) Funds	DO ACDO	£ 3,300	1.7.71	31.12.71	Necessary funds for 11 Dips collected (£ 6,000/— per dip)
b) Materials	ACDO Dip Committee		1.10.71	30.4.72	Materials for 11 dips on site
c) Labour	ACDO	C. D. Staff	1.8.71	31.5.72	Labour for 11 dips provided

Notes:
1. See Appendix E for Annual Programming Chart for this project showing progress at the end of November 1971 and Appendix F for the Monthly Management Report for November 1971.
2. The actual APF continues on a second sheet.

Appendix E

Annual Programming Chart

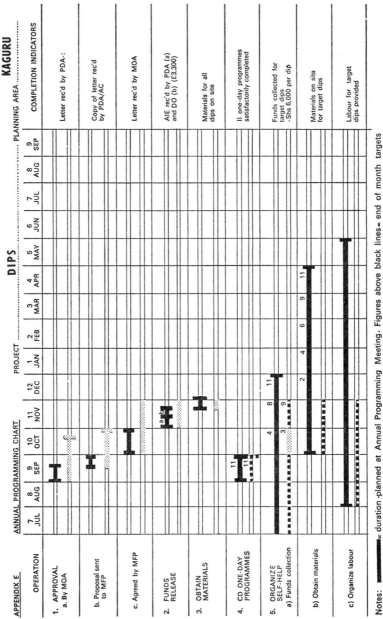

Appendix F

Specimen Monthly Management Report

MONTHLY MANAGEMENT REPORT FOR KAGURU DIVISION FOR NOVEMBER 1971
Based on the meeting held in the Area Co-ordinator's Operations Room on Tuesday 30 November 1971.

Present
(Name) District Officer, Chairman
   ,,   Assistant Agricultural Officer, Kaguru
   ,,   Assistant Community Development Officer
   ,,   Assistant Co-operative Officer
   ,,   District Range Officer
   ,,   Superintendent, Roads
   ,,   Livestock Marketing Officer
   ,,   District Livestock Officer
   ,,   Assistant Livestock Officer
   ,,   Health Inspector
   ,,   Area Co-ordinator, Secretary

Next Meeting: Wednesday 29th December at 9.00 a.m. in the Area Co-ordinator's Operations Room.

PROGRESS AND ACTION SUMMARY

Project/ Operation	Target by 30.11.71	Actual at 30.11.71	On time	Action required	
				Action	by
Dips					
1.c. Agreed by MFP	Letter rec'd by MOA by 31.10	Not yet rec'd	No	Expedite	MFP
2. Funds Release	AIE for £3,300 rec'd by PDA and DLO	Not yet rec'd	No	See 1.c.	MFP/ MOA

Project/ Operation	Target by 30.11.71	Actual at 30.11.71	On time	Action required Action	by
5.a. Organize self-help funds collection	Complete for 8 dips	Complete for 9 dips	Yes	Continue	DO ACDO
b. Obtain self-help materials	In hand	In hand	Yes	Continue	ACDO
c. Organize self-help labour	In hand	In hand	Yes	Continue	ACDO
Maize Credit					
3.c. Approval by AFC of loanees	AFC HQ approvals for 900 acres rec'd by AFC Branch Manager	Not yet rec'd	No	Expedite	AFC HQ

etc. etc. (additional projects)

PROGRESS AND PROBLEMS

Dips

Self-help contributions have improved. 9 dip committees have completed collection of Shs 6,000 each, one more than the end-of-month target. Obtaining self-help materials is well in hand for all dips and local enthusiasm is so high that organizing labour poses no problems.

Construction due to begin on 1 December is now held up by the release of funds. MOA has approved but MFP approval is still awaited. If funds are not released soon, the entire construction programme will be delayed and the local staff will be demoralized, having promised the dip committees that government would act as soon as their collections were complete. Early action requested.

MFP and then MOA, PDA, LO

Maize Credit

This project in which a great deal of staff time has been invested and which has roused the hopes of some 450 farmers, many of whom have prepared their land, will have to be abandoned if the AFC HQ approvals are not received by the AFC Branch Manager by 10 December, as the rains and planting will not wait. Even if the authority is received by 10 December, it will be very difficult to get the seeds and fertilizer to the farmers on time. Etc., etc., (additional projects).

PROJECT PREPARATION

Family Planning

A draft workplan for 1972 is being prepared by the Provincial Medical Officer with the assistance of the Area Officer, Family Planning Association, for the experimental family planning/rural health project. Funds for this project were included in the 1972/73 Draft Estimates proposals. The workplan runs from February 1972 to June 1976. It will be considered at the next MMM on 29 December 1971. Etc., etc., (additional projects).

OTHER MATTERS

DISTRIBUTION

Appendix G

Instructions for the Assistant Agricultural Officer in charge of a division on operating the management system for crops staff

Purpose

The purpose of the management system is to improve crop extension work by:

(i) providing a routine for co-ordinated planning of work
(ii) giving you more effective operational control over staff activities
(iii) providing you with regular feedback on an individual basis on what staff members have been doing
(iv) improving staff motivation and performance through a combination of supervision and of encouraging them to take a responsible part in drawing up systematic work programmes

Method

The central feature of the method is a monthly management meeting held by you in each location with the locational crops staff. There are five components in the full system:

1. A *Daily Activities Record* (DAR) kept by each staff member. This shows the days of the month, the number of days available for extension work, the extension activities planned for the period with targets, the work carried out each day recorded on a daily basis, and a summary of achievement and the number of farmers advised by the end of the period. It provides each staff member with a work plan and targets for the month, and provides you with a record of what is reported to have been done by the end of the period.

2. A *Location Planning Sheet* (LPS) worked out by you and the LAA in charge of the location. This shows the number of days available for extension work for each staff member in the location, and enables you to list and place in order of priority the various extension activities to be carried out, and to assign these and agree them with staff so that their work loads are realistic.

3. A *Black Book* maintained by each staff member listing by village or other grouping those farmers whom he visits and the date of each visit. The dates of successive visits are written across the page so that you can easily see how frequently a farmer has been visited.

4. A *Farm Visit Book* (the Red Book), held by each farmer who receives visits, and in which the staff member records his visit, the advice given, and any comments.

5. The *Daily Diary* kept by each staff member.

The recommended sequence for introducing the system is to begin with the monthly meeting, the DAR and the LPS and operate these for three months. Then the Black Book and the Farm Visit Books can be added. A Staff Activities Summary is an extra part of the system which should only be added if you wish it for your own purposes or if the information on it is required and used by the District Agricultural Officer. The instructions which follow are for the full system without the Staff Activities Summary. If that is used, be careful that completing it does not distract you or the LAA from the main work of the meeting. It may be best for it to be made out after the meeting. The instructions assume that the staff members are familiar with the DAR. When introducing the system, it should be explained to them carefully and they should have plenty of opportunity to practice with the form.

HOW TO HOLD THE MONTHLY MANAGEMENT MEETING

Before the meeting

- arrange the date and place of the meeting
- inform the DAO of the date and place (in case he wishes to attend, and so that he can take steps to avoid other commitments for you on that date)
- obtain information needed for planning the next month's work, including date of pay, visits, meetings, etc.
- avoid other commitments on the day of the meeting

At the meeting

(i) *Debriefing:* With the LAA sit down with each staff member in turn. Examine his DAR, Diary and Black Book. Discuss in detail the work he has done. Encourage him to explain problems he has encountered. Compare the targets which were set the month before with his actual performance. Where they have been achieved, circle them in green.

Where they have not been achieved, circle them in red. Encourage honest reporting by understanding the difficulties encountered. Make some cross checks between the DAR, Diary and Black Book.

(ii) *Discussion:* When the debriefing is complete, discuss any general matters of the sort which are normally reserved for monthly meetings. A separate monthly meeting should not be necessary.

(iii) *Joint Planning:* Decide the date of the next meeting and complete the top section of the LPS. At the same time, staff members should complete the top part of their DARs. You should all then be agreed on the number of days available for work. (Treat Saturdays as half-days.)

On the LPS list the crops, crop operations and extension methods for the coming month, and then place these in order of priority by entering numbers in the left hand column. Enter targets where these are predetermined (e.g., for demonstrations).

Now, in discussion with the staff, allocate to them those targets which have had to be predetermined. The allocations are written on the left hand side of their columns on the LPS. On the right hand side of their columns write in the number of work days required.

Continue with the top priority operations. Keep a running total of days remaining for allocation for each staff member. When the centrally determined and top priority operations have been allocated, tell each staff member how many days he has left and ask him how, given the conditions and needs of his area, he thinks they should be spent. His participation at this stage is important, and he should have a genuine sense that he can and does take part in determining his work and targets. (If all the days are to be spent on farm visits, you can give him a target number of visits, perhaps at 3 or 4 a day, and ask him to suggest how these should be divided between different crops.)

When these work targets have been agreed, all the days available for work should have been allocated.

Each staff member should have recorded the operations and targets on his DAR which he then takes with him as a guide and record until the following meeting.

Between meetings

LAAs should as usual supervise the work of JAAs, and should check Farm Visit Books, DARs and Black Books to ensure that these are being maintained correctly.

192

LOCATION PLANNING SHEET (LPS)   LOCATION.............. FROM.......... TO......... (inclusive)TOTAL DAYS....................

Complete this part before monthly meeting	Sub-location															
	Staff member															
																TOTALS
	Week-ends/Pub.Hols															
	Leave															
	Pay/Office Work															
	Official Meetings															
	Courses/Shows															
	Total days committed															
	Working days available															

Priority	Crop	Crop Operation	Ext MTD	Target											

WHEN COMPLETE TRANSFER PLANNED FIGURES TO STAFF ACTIVITIES SHEET

EXTENSION AGENT'S DAILY ACTIVITY RECORD (DAR)   NAME............... SUBLOCATION.......... FROM...... TO.....inclusive TOTAL DAYS.....

Use pencil to plan. Enter actual in ink		PLANNED		Actual
	Weekends/Pub.Hols.			
	Leave			
	Pay/Office Work			
	Official Meetings			
	Courses/Shows			
	Total			

Days planned available for extension =   Less   =
Days actually available for extension =   Less   =

Priority	Crop	Crop Operation	Ext MTD	Target		Actual

Farmers Advised - Totals -

Above enter number of farmers advised

Abbreviate crop operations and extension methods e.g. W=weeding A=agric.Baraza D=demonstration FV=farm visit

Complete after work every day

193

13 — Managing Rural Development

Appendix H

Instructions for a District Livestock Officer or Livestock Officer on operating the management system for livestock staff

Purpose

The purpose of the management system is to improve staff effectiveness by:

(i)   providing a routine for co-ordinated planning of work
(ii) giving you more effective operational control over staff activities
(iii) providing you with regular feedback on an individual basis on what staff members have been doing
(iv) improving staff motivation and performance through a combination of supervision and of encouraging them to take a responsible part in drawing up systematic work programmes
(v)   simplifying reports and making them easier to handle

Method

The central feature of the method is a monthly management meeting held by you in each location with the locational livestock staff. The meeting centres around the Work Plan and Report Form of each livestock staff member. This form has two functions:

(i)   to provide a means for planning work and recording work done
(ii) to provide a streamlined and standardized means of reporting information required.

The diaries kept by staff are also an important part of the meeting.

Before the meeting

- arrange the date and place of the meeting
- inform the district level staff who need to know (DAO, DAHO, DVO, DAI Officer, etc.)
- obtain full details from those officers of any campaigns planned and any dates and places for required attendance by staff
- find out the dates of pay for the coming month (both central government and County Council, as necessary)
- avoid all other commitments on the day of the meeting

At the meeting

(i) *Debriefing:* With the supervisory staff sit down with each staff member in turn. Examine his Daily Work Plan and Report Form for the past month and also his Diary. Discuss in detail the work he has done. Encourage him to explain problems he has encountered. Compare the targets which were set the month before with his actual performance. Make some cross-checks between the Diary and the Daily Work Plan and Report Form.

(ii) *Discussion:* When the debriefing is complete, discuss any general matters of the sort which are normally reserved for monthly meetings. A separate monthly meeting should not be necessary.

(iii) *Joint Planning:* Now, with the staff, plan the coming month. Decide the date of the next meeting.

Each staff member now completes the top line and the date and day columns of his Form for the next period. "Sundays" and "Public Holidays" should be entered in the "Planned" column where appropriate.

Each staff member then fills in the "Planned" column with commitments in this sequence:

(i)   leave, courses and pay
(ii) centrally planned campaigns for which dates have been decided
(iii) routine activities such as dip or market attendance
(iv) barazas, meetings and demonstrations

The days remaining are then added up and entered in the box indicated by the arrow.

For the days remaining, activities and their priorities are listed. Ask

195

staff members to make suggestions based on their local knowledge and to suggest how their time should be allocated between activities. Discuss these suggestions and agree an allocation of days and targets.

At the bottom right hand corner of the form enter the headings for any data to be reported.

Each staff member should then leave the meeting with his Form as a record of agreed action for the coming period, and should keep it up to date daily.

Between Meetings

Staff should be supervised as normal, and the Forms and Diaries should be checked to see that they are being kept correctly.

DISEASE OUTBREAK

Date	Old or New	Disease	Place	No. of cases recorded	No. of innoculations	Other action taken

INNOCULATIONS ADMINISTERED	No. of animals	No. of doses	No. of doses wasted	A.I. cattle	Total	CASTRATIONS			
				Calves born		Bulls		Boars	
				Offspring deaths		Billies		Dogs	
				Living offspring		Rams		Donkeys	

LIVESTOCK MOVEMENTS

	Numbers	From where	To where	Details (thefts, sales etc)
Imports				
Exports				

PROGRESS WITH NEW DIPS

Name	Shillings collected		Stage reached/Remarks
	This month	Total	

PROGRESS WITH EXISTING DIPS

Name	No. of dippings	No. of cattle equivalents*	Gallons added dawa:water	Date of testing	Action taken	Comments (cleaning & filling etc)

*5 Sheep or Goats = 1 Cow

DEMONSTRATION AND BARAZAS

Date	Place	B or D	No. of farmers	Purpose	Comments

B=Baraza D=Demonstration

GENERAL Forage condition, Weather, Visitors, Problems, Other

DAILY WORK PLAN AND REPORT FORM FOR LIVESTOCK STAFF

NAME:_____ (SUB-)LOCATION:_____ FROM: _____ TO:_____

Date	Day	Planned	Actual	1.	2.	3

Days remaining (1 1/2 day for Saturday)= _____   Total

Plan for days remaining by priority		Planned Days	Actual Days	Total farmers advised	
					1=
					2=
					3=

198

Abbreviations

AA	Agricultural Assistant
AAO	Assistant Agricultural Officer
ACDO	Assistant Community Development Officer
AHA	Animal Husbandry Assistant
DAHO	District Animal Husbandry Officer
DAI Officer	District Artificial Insemination Officer
DAR	Daily Activities Record
DDC	District Development Committee
DVO	District Veterinary Officer
FAO	Food and Agriculture Organization of the United Nations
IDS	Institute for Development Studies, University of Nairobi
ILO	International Labour Organization of the United Nations
JAA	Junior Agricultural Assistant
JAHA	Junior Animal Husbandry Assistant
LAA	Locational Agricultural Assistant
LPS	Location Planning Sheet
MBO	Management by Objectives
MP	Member of Parliament
NORAD	Norwegian Agency for International Development
O and M	Organization and Methods
PDC	Provincial Development Committee
PIM	Programming and Implementation Management
R and D	Research and Development
RDC	Regional Development Committee
RDF	Regional Development Fund
SIDA	Swedish International Development Authority
SRDP	Special Rural Development Programme (Kenya)
UN	United Nations
UNITAR	United Nations Institute for Training and Research

Index

This index, alphabetically ordered, is primarily designed as a functional guide to information. Major references are in **boldface** type, quotes in *italics*. The preface and appendices are not included; a complete listing of the technical literature is given in the References (pp. 165—175). The Index has been compiled by David Minugh.

programming meetings
disease, control of plant 130, **136**
-free seed-breeding 131
treatment of human and animal
130
See also dips; health
dispensaries 102
District, Agricultural Officer 66, 67
Commissioner 87, 89
Councils 86
Development and Planning Committee 89
Development Committee 85, **87**, 89, 90, 91, 92—3, 94, 96, 97, 99
Development Director 19
Development Officer, see Area Co-ordinator
Development Secretary, see Area Co-ordinator
Director of Development, see Area Co-ordinator
Governors 87, 89
Officers I, see Area Co-ordinator
Planning Officer, see Area Co-ordinator
Team and Planning Committee 90, 91, 92
Dodoma (Tanzania) 141, 145
donor agency 15, 21, **29**, 39, 115, 116, 119
drinking 57, 123, see also staff, criticism of field
DVO, see veterinary services (District Veterinary Officer)

Eastern Africa, budgets 17
population, percent rural 12
ecological succession 131—2
zones 138—9
econometric model-building 115, 116, 118
Economic Planning and Development, Ministry of (Kenya) 20, see also Planning, Ministry of
economists 13, 29, 31, 114, 132, 152
agricultural 116, 138, **147**, 148, 161
and planning 19, 22, 114, **116**, 117, 118, 137—8

research 147
economy, cash 111, 114, 115
general 116
subsistence 114
education 14, 17, 55, 86, 111
colonial 22
for farm children 79
for staff children 23, 159
primary 18
See also schools
effects, unanticipated of programmes 123
efficiency, staff time 25, see also staff, field
elite, local 88, **109—10**
counteracting **110—112**
See also participation, local; social pressure, staff and local elite
Embu District (Kenya) 65
empirical development **150—1**
employment, rural 123, 130
engineering 129
engineers 137
electrical 28
roads 28
water 28, 107
equipment 122
heavy 122
ploughing 120
equity **79—83**
and participation **108—113**
and politics 82—3
and research and development **136—7**
See also bias
erosion, see soil erosion
Ethiopia 15, 16, etc.
Chilalo Agricultural Development Unit (CADU) 15, 16, 119—20
ethnic groups 87, 102
networks for promotions 63, see also self-help
evaluation 19, 27, 33, 34, **53**, **118—28**, 148, 157—8, 161
delays in **125**
evaluators and **124—6**
ex post **28—9**, 118—9
history of **119—21**

204

internal 126—9
methodology of 121—4
purposes of 125
self-evaluation 40
staff 63, 75, 76, 78, 159, see also
    meetings, monthly systems of
    122
See also evaluators; mission eva-
    luation officer; Reviews
evaluators as academics 125
    as parasites 125
    as participants 126
    as resource 126
    experience and motivation of 124
    for IDS 120—1
    implementors 124
    self-discipline for 124—5
    staff as 128, 129
    values of 124
executive capacity 17—18, 141—2
exchange, foreign 13
expatriates, see staff (foreign v. na-
    tional)
experimental method 121—2
export crops 13, see also crops
extension, see agricultural research
    and extension; farm visits

factory 41
family living, better 72
family planning, see planning, family
FAO, see Food and Agricultural Or-
    ganization of the United Nations
farm credit 44
    development 79
    large-scale 144
    management experiment 44
    small 131
    visits 57—8, 61, 67—8, 69—71,
        82
        book, see book, red; location
            register
        ritual 74
farmers 75, 79—83, 134, 136
    as information source 134—6
    poorer 80—1, 83, 148
    progressive 58, 79, 83, 111
    small 147
    training 44, 81, 122, 126

young, club, see young farmers'
    club
See also bias toward richer far-
    mers; peasant conservatism
feedback, see information flow
fertilizer 59, 120, 131, 132
    demonstrations 44, 67
field trials 133, see also agricultural
    research and extension
field programmes 29, see also pro-
    grammes
field staff, see staff, field
Finance, Ministry of 61, 98
    Committee of (Uganda) 97
fisheries 55
fish ponds 98
flood control 98
Food and Agriculture Organization
    of the United Nations (FAO)
    at Migori 142
    with SRDP and SIDA 21
    See also United Nations
forced labour, see labour, forced
foreign aid 144, see also donor agen-
    cy
foreigners, see staff (foreign v. na-
    tional); universities; Institute for
    Development Studies
forestry 17, 55
functional literacy, see literacy, func-
    tional
funds for staff (petrol) 37
    inefficient spending 17
    releases 20, 45, 51, 103
    See also allocations; block grants;
        delays in fund releasing

game 55, 144
garages 95
Geita District Plan (Tanz.) 142,
    143
geologists 135
Gezira (Sudan) 15, 16
goals, changing 111—2, 123
    in SRDP 123
government, local, see participation,
    local
government structures 26

new 26
grants, block, see block grants
Great Britain, ODA and SRDP 21
Groundnut Scheme (Tanz.) 15
grazing resources 109
groups, see churches; clubs; committees; ethnic groups; interest groups; religious groups; self-help

Harambee settlement scheme (Kenya) 83, 101, 102—3, 103
health 14, 18, 55, 86, 101, 102, 109, 112
   centre construction 44
   clinic, mobile 44
   facilities 17, 26, *35*, 87, 102, 110
health staff, see staff, health
Hiding Hand principle (Hirschman) 104
Highlands, (former) White (Kenya) 116
hierarchies, structural 55, see also administration, authoritarian
Holland, and SRDP 21
home economics 17, 26, 44, 112
   Home Economics Assistant 80
hotels 95
housing 44
   for staff 37, 59, 61, 159
   See also staff, field, terms of service
"hub-and-wheel" systems 32
human relations school 32
hubrids (seeds) 137, see also maize, hybrid

IDS, see Institute for Development Studies
ignorance, optimal 153, 156, see also information, excessive
ILO, see International Labour Organization of the United Nations
implementation 27—9, 31, 33, 34, 36—7, 127, see also programming; Programming and Implementation Managing System; Review, Annual Implementation
income, minimum rural 12
   (ILO) 81

indicators of achievement 119, 122
   proxy 155
   social 119
industrialization 13
information, caveats on 75
   delays 47, 125, **127—8**
   essential 145
   flow **66**, 67, 76, **77**, 127, 133, **138—9**
   inaccurate 40, 41, 66, 74, 116, 139, 156
   oversophisticated 117, 125, 129, 147
   useless collection of 19, 32—3, 37, 40, 41, **50**, 64, **68**, 128, 136, 141, **142—3**, 144, **150**, **153**, 161
inoculation (livestock) 66, 71
input, types **122**, see also evaluation, systems of
insemination 71
inspection, disruptive **72—3**
   from higher levels 23, **60**
   See also staff, field, supervision of
Institute for Development Research (Copenhagen) 143
Institute for Development Studies (IDS) 120, 138, see also University of Nairobi
institutes of technology, see technology, institutes of
"integrated" rural development (UN) **24—6**
integration, of rural development **24**, 25—6, see also co-ordination
Intensive Development Zone Programme (Zambia) 117
   evaluation of 127
interest groups 85, 88, 102, see also groups
International Labour Organization of the United Nations (ILO) 81, 98, 139
   report on Kenya (1972) 12
investment, rural, see rural development
investors, foreign, see donor agency
Irianyi, and SRDP 142
irrigation scheme 123

JAA, see Agricultural Assistants, Junior
JAHA, see Animal Husbandry Assistant, Junior
joint programming, see programming, joint
joint target-setting, see targets
Journal of Administration Overseas 86
Junior Agricultural Assistant, see Agricultural Officer, Assistant
Junior Animal Husbandry Assistant, see Animal Husbandry Assistant

Kapenguria (Kenya), SRDP and Holland 21
Karonga (Malawi) and World Bank 15
Katumani maize, see maize, Katumani
Kaunda, Dr. Kenneth, President, Republic of Zambia 11, *12*
Kenya Institute of Administration 42
Kenya, Republic of 11, 12, etc.
  budget 29, **30**
  Conference at Kericho 20
  Development Plan (1970—74) 11, 141
  Directorate of Personnel Management, President's Office 160
  ILO Mission to (1972) 12
  Million Acre Settlement Scheme 15
  Mwea Irrigation Scheme 15
  National Irrigation Board 15
  rural population, percent 12
  settlement schemes 56, 83
  See also PIM; SRDP; Tetu; University of Nairobi
Kenya Tea Development Authority **62**, see also tea extension
Kericho, conference at (1966) 20
Khama, Sir Seretse, President, Republic of Botswana 11, *12*
Kiharu and SRDP 142
Kilimanjaro District plan 142, 143
Kisii District (Kenya) 102, 111
kitchens, building 101

Kitui and SRDP 142
  and NORAD 143
knowledge, local **134—6**
  of soils and vegetation **134—5**
  of weather **134**
Kwale (Kenya), SRDP and ODA (Great Britain) 21

LAA, see Agricultural Assistants, Locational
labour, forced 103
  seasonal 147
  unexploited 13, 100
land 55
  adjudication 44, 144
  licensing 86
  purchase 79
  reform 109
  settlement scheme 41
  underdeveloped 154
  unsettled 83
  use choices 144
leaders', locational, seminars, see locational leaders' seminars
lead time for fund release 45, see also funds
Leonard Principle 75, 82
Lesotho 54, 79
liaison between levels of government 118
licensing bicycles 109
  businesses 86
  land plots 86
Lilongwe (Malawi) and World Bank 15
linear programming, see programming, linear
literacy, adult 17
  functional 72
  staff 67, 69
livestock 65—6, 71, 103, 109, 116, 131, see also castration; cattle, grade; census (livestock); inocculation (livestock); staff, field; staff, livestock
living allowance, see allowance
living, better family, see family living, better
loans 122

local elite, see elite local

government, see participation, local

interest groups, see interest groups, local

knowledge, see knowledge, local

participation, see participation, local

Locational Agricultural Assistant (LAA) **65**, 66, 84, see also Agricultural Assistants

locational monthly meeting, see meetings

Location Planning Sheet **69**, 70, see also appendix, p. 193

location register 67

and future planning 77

See also farm visits; book, black

LPS, see Location Planning Sheet

Lusaka (Zambia) 21, 117

Lutosho Integrated Rural Development Programme (Tanz.) 126

McNamara, Robert (World Bank) 12

mabati groups 101, 111, see also women's groups

Maendeleo ya Wanawake, see women's groups

maize and beans 131

composite 132

hybrid 81, 122, 130, 132

Katumani 65

Malawi 15, 18, etc.

Development Committees 18

malnutrition 123

Malaysia, operations room concept 42

programme bias in 41

red book system 42, 53

management advisory services 31

authoritarian, see administration, authoritarian

Management by Objectives (MBO) 42, 68, 74, 75, 155

management control of self-help groups 102

meetings 43, **46**, *51*, 53, 67, **155—6**, see also App. B; PIM

procedures 32, 39, **52—3**, 65,

144—5, 149

report, see report, action

systems, abolishment of old **157**

genesis of 21

improving 27, 41, **113**, 149, **158—9**, 160

of field staff 33, 34, **62—4**, **162**

principles of **149—55**

specialists in 31

See also MBO; systems analysis

managers, see evaluators; planners; staff

manpower, shortage of high-level African **22—3**, 144, see also staff (foreign *v.* national)

resources 159

Mao, Chairman *123*

marketing 14

markets 86, 147

materials, see resources

maximizing, see optimizing

Mbere (Kenya), description of **65**, 134

ecological mapping of 138—9

plans of 141

SRDP 72

SRDP and NORAD 21

MBO, see Management By Objectives

medicine 129

meetings, joint programming, see programming exercise

limiting attendance at 44, 46, **49—50**

monthly (for planning) 67, **68**, **70—1**, **71—3**

openness at **44**, 46, 49, **155—6**

public 85

reasons for **156**

wasteful 37, **49—50**, 53, **89—94**, 156

See also development committees; management meetings; participation, local

Member of Parliament 91, 93, 97

metrological data 139, see also rainfall stations

Mexico 142 peabeans 65

Migori (Kenya) 84

and FAO 142
and SRDP and SIDA (and FAO) 21
Million-Acre Settlement Scheme (Kenya) 15
minimum extension package programme 16, **120**, see also CADU
mining 13
Ministry of, see Agriculture, Ministry of, Finance, Ministry of, etc.
mission evaluation officer 119, see also evaluators
models, econometric, see econometric models
ideal 150—1
monitoring 28—9, 31
system (bar-chart), see bar-chart monitoring system
monthly management report, see report, action
motorcycles 59, 60
MP, see Member of Parliament
Mubuku Irrigation Scheme (Uganda) 15
multi-sector bounded-site programmes and projects 14, **15—7**, 21—2, 31
Mwanza (Tanzania) 141
Regional Development Committee 89
Mwea Irrigation Scheme (Kenya) 15, 31
Settlement Scheme 62
Myrdal, Gunnar *124*

Nachingwea mechanized settlement scheme 15
Nairobi, University of, see University of Nairobi
Narok District (Kenya) 144
National Development Plan, see Botswana, Republic of
National Irrigation Board (Kenya) 15
Ndegwa Commission (Kenya) 39, 92, 100, 154
network analysis 42
diagram 41
Nigeria 59, 62

Nigerian Tobacco Company 62, see also tobacco extension
NORAD, see Norwegian Agency for International Development
North Nardi (Kenya) 142
Norway, see Norwegian Agency for International Development
Norwegian Agency for International Development (NORAD) 143
and SRDP 21
nutrition 17, 26, 112, 133
Nyakashaka settlement for schoolleavers (Uganda) 15, 16
Nyerere, Mwalimu Julius, President, United Republic of Tanzania *11*, 12, *36*, 110—1, *114*, 161
Nyeri (Kenya) 111

ODA, see Great Britain
Okovanga Swamp (Botswana) 131
"On Time", see report, action
operations room, use in planning 42, **45—6**
opportunity-orientation **153—4**
optimal ignorance **153**, see also information, excessive
optimizing 25, **152—3**
organization theory 161, see also management systems
outputs, types of **122**, see also evaluation, systems of

package, input 81, see also minimum extension package programme
paddy-growing 16, 62, see also Mwea Settlement Scheme
paperwork, see information, useless collection of; reports, excessive
parastatals 17, 22, 26
Parliament, Member of 91, 93, 97
participation 100, **108—13**
in planning 72
local 33, 34, 55, 84, 161, 162
analysis of **85—6**, 113
definitions of **85**
history of **86—88**
inequal 109
See also elite, local; equity; knowledge, local; self-help

parties, political, see political parties
pathologists, plant 136, see also diseases, plant
patronage, see block grants, political
PDC, see Provincial Development Committee
peabeans (Mexico 142) 65
peasant conservatism **60—1**, 130, 154, see also farmers
perfectionism, see empirical development
petrol, funds for 37
phasing form **45—6**, 48—9, see also App. D, p. 185
pilot experiment 27, 157—8
Pilot Village Settlements, post-Independence (Tanz.) 15
PIM, see Programming and Implementation Management
pipeline construction 104
plan formulation 28—9, 31, 33, 34, 141, 145—6, 159, 161
    useless 19—20, **139—46**
    See also area plan information
  long-term national 11
  management, progressive **145**
planners 114—148
  and local staff **144**
  as a resource **114**, 116, **146—8**, 150, 156
  criticism by **116**
  criticism of **114—5**, 117, **148**
  definition of 114
  field occupations of **118**
  jealousy of **115**
  managing **146—8**
  nationality of 114, 115, 116, 117, **143**, 160—1
  occupations of 116
  practical *v.* theoretical **115—6**, see also empirical development
  See also staff
planning **28—9**
  family 14, 17, 26, 72, 112
  for planners **146—8**
  management of, actual **117—8**
  models of **118**, 147
  theoretical *v.* practical **115—6**
  work, see work planning

See also crop staff planning; livestock staff planning
Planning Division (Kenya) 116
Planning, Ministry of
  in Kenya 19, 20, 92
  in Tanzania 19
  in Uganda 92
  in Zambia 19
  Note: full titles vary
plantations 15
planting 131, 132
ploughing equipment 120
political parties 85, 87, 88, 89, 97, 110
  pressures 29, 125, 148
  relationships 121
  representation 89
  stability 87
  support from the people 85, 89
  support from higher levels 16, 42—3, **54**, **82—3**, 159
political scientists 55, 115
politics in block grants **97**, 98, see also block grants
"pombe parties" 57, see also staff, field, criticism of; drinking
population density (Kenya) 20
  growth 145
  percent rural 12
postal service 89
poverty, rural 12, **80—1**, 112
  urban 12
PPBS, see Programme Planning and Budgeting Systems
Practical Concepts Incorporated 119
price control 91
  supports 13
Princeton and IDS 120, 143
priority, determining 145
  importance of 66, **67**
  shifts in **118**
  See also target; work planning
problem orientation **153—4**
  rural 12, **22—7**
  solving **153—4**
  See also: agricultural research and extension; administration, authoritative; staff weaknesses; area plan formulation, problems

Development Director 19
Development Fund (Tanz.) 19, **95—7**, 99, 108
See also block grants; development committees
register, location, see location, register
small, see book, black
religious groups 102, see also groups
remedial action, see action, remedial
reorganization **26—7**, see also decentralization
replicability 19, 21, **120**, 138
from pilot projects **157—8**
report, action 43, **47—8**, 48—9, **50**, 73
as an operational control 47
distribution of 47
and estimate preparation **127—9**
colonial 119
distribution of 47, 156
excessive 37, **50**, 53, 68, 77, 156, see plan formation, useless
monthly, see action report
ritual 40, 50, 64, 127, 128, 156
simplifying 68, 73, 77, **78—9**, 128
See also App. C.
reporting, costs of 77
system of **39—41**, 67, 73, 77, 129
research and development 83, 158, 160
accuracy and relevance of **139**
agricultural, see agricultural research and development
and equity 112, **136—7**
and farmers **136—7**
designs, inappropriate **131**
diversity of **129—130**
information exchange 136, 161
mapping ecological zones 138—9
organization of **137—9**
rural 33, 34, **129—39**, 148, 157, 161, 162
resources 145, 152
advantages of **144—5**
grazing 109
inadequate 37, **51**
local **86**
manpower 159, see also planners

as a resource
use strategy **142—5**, 145
water 109
responsibility and Area Co-ordinator 39
revenue collection 86, see also tax collection
Review, Annual Evaluation 127, **128**, 129
Annual Implementation **127**
Half-Yearly 127, **128**
roads 14, 17, 18, 86, 96
access 110
construction 44, 93, 98, 108, 122
engineer, see engineer, road
engineering 23
maintenance 93
Rungwe District plan (Tanz.) 142, 143
rural bias, see bias, rural
development 33, 152
analysis of **147**, 151
evaluation of **119—20**
Rural Development Plan 97
priority of 12—3
employment 14
investment 13
population, percent 12
problems 12, see also problems

saturation, in Canadian civil service 158
school 87, 101, 102, **104**
nursery 110
primary 110
secondary 87, 110, 111
school-leavers 15, 16, 123, 130
seasonal labour, see labour, seasonal
Second National Development Plan (Zambia) *11*, *84*, 141
Second World War 13
sector, definition 14
sectoral, definition 14
programme 14, **17—18**, 22, 32
seeds 59, 60, 67, 120, 130, 137
breeding 131
See also maize, hybrid
self-evaluation, see evaluation
self-help 16, 41, 44, 72, 87, 88, 98,

213